Redesign © 2019
Previously published in 2012 as "Growing Your Own Ve[g]"
by

**Royal
Botanic Garden
Edinburgh**

20A Inverleith Row, Edinburgh EH3 5LR, UK

ISBN: 978-1-910877-31-9

The Royal Botanic Garden Edinburgh (RBGE) is a charity registered in Scotland (number SC007983) and is supported by the Scottish Government Rural and Environmental Science and Analytical Services.

Please be aware of anything which may cause allergies or adverse reactions when preparing any food in our recipes.
Always wash food well and be sure you have identified any parts of the plant correctly before eating.

Contributors: Ben Dell, Jenny Foulkes, Erica Randall
Editors: Alice Young (original), Donna Cole and Simon Spanton (revised)
Layout: Caroline Muir

The publisher wishes to acknowledge the support of the players of People's Postcode Lottery towards the publication of this book.

Supported by players of

PEOPLE'S POSTCODE LOTTERY

Awarded funds from

POSTCODE EARTH TRUST

Printed by Ivanhoe Caledonian Printing Company Ltd

FSC
MIX
Paper from responsible sources
FSC® C022665
www.fsc.org

Foreword

It's a great pleasure to be able to welcome you to Edible Gardening in Scotland, a revised and updated edition of Growing Your Own Vegetables. Since its original publication in 2011 the increased understanding of the benefits to both physical and mental health of growing and eating your own produce has made the information and encouragement in these pages ever more timely. A key aim of our Edible Gardening Project is to share horticultural knowledge and to promote growing your own vegetables, so we're delighted to be able to present this handy and practical distillation of the experiences and learning of the staff, students and volunteers here at the Botanic Garden who have, over the years, embraced the challenges and opportunities of growing your own vegetables.

Whether in a garden or an allotment or in containers and window boxes, growing your own vegetables provides proven benefits relating to contact with the natural world; mindfulness, exercise, learning or simply time spent outside. And, of course, the benefits only begin with the growing; reaching your five a day when you have perhaps grown some of them yourself is all the more satisfying. It's an activity that also presents, whatever the weather and the results, wonderful opportunities for bringing together generations and social groups in a shared and cooperative endeavour. Happy gardening, and good eating!

Simon Milne MBE, Regius Keeper

Contents

Introduction

Growing and eating your own vegetables is a very rewarding experience. Spending your time outside tending them reconnects you with what you are eating as well as being a therapeutic pastime. Come harvest time there is a huge feeling of accomplishment and eating the very freshest of food from your garden means better taste and less of an impact on the environment. With a few basic techniques, producing fresh, nutritious crops can be easy whatever your available time and space.

The combination of location, soil and conditions makes the situation in your garden unique. This book will help you plan around these factors, offer inspiration and ideas for making the most of the space you have and guide you through the basic principles of growing the vegetables you like to eat.

Know your plot

Before starting to grow, get to know your garden by watching it or taking photographs throughout the day (ideally at different times of the year) to see which areas get the most sun and shade. Here are the main things to consider.

Site

Soil conditions

Soil is your most important asset for growing. Knowing what you have in terms of soil pH, texture and structure will determine what you can grow. There are ways to improve your soil (see pp. 37–40).

Site aspect

The direction your garden faces affects how much sunshine it receives. A south-facing garden is ideal for growing the widest range of crops, although some plants benefit from part-shade and a few even cope with a north-facing aspect. As long as your garden is not heavily shaded by buildings or trees, plants will receive reasonably high light levels regardless of the aspect.

Landscape

A flat site is the easiest for everyday growing and maintenance. Gardens on steep slopes may need terracing to prevent soil erosion. Slopes can also create frost pockets where the cold air sinks and stays at the lowest point.

Weather

Rainfall

The average monthly rainfall will depend greatly on where you live. As a general rule southern and eastern regions of the UK are the driest, while the further west and north you live the wetter it becomes.

Wind

Wind has a strong drying and chilling effect and can flatten or snap the stems of taller crops. In coastal regions salt-laden winds are extremely damaging to plants. The main solution is semi-permeable windbreaks, which filter and slow down wind movement. A solid barrier can channel the air current over the top and create turbulence on the opposite side.

Windbreaks

Living windbreaks made from plants, hedges or trees look good but can compete with your crops for light, water and nutrients if close to the growing area.

Artificial windbreaks – wooden fences or plastic web or mesh – are efficient but expensive, and are not so aesthetically pleasing.

Temperature

Seeds and plants rarely grow below 5°C and suffer if temperatures are above 25°C. Temperature, along with daylight hours, affects the 'growing season' – the period between the last frost in spring and the first frosts in autumn, when plants are actively growing. Depending on where you live in the UK this can vary widely and can change from year to year because of changes in weather patterns.

Most seed packets and gardening books give growing instructions for the whole of the UK. With some experience and a little know-how gardeners can adapt this information to their particular site.

So, if you live in the far north or at high altitudes you will need to adjust the prescribed sowing and planting dates accordingly. In the far north this may be up to four weeks later. The season also starts two weeks later for every 300m increase in elevation, because as the location becomes higher it will become colder.

Other temperature factors to take into account:

- Sheltered gardens (especially south- or south-west-facing) can become suntraps on hot days. Excessive heat can scorch and wilt plants.
- Inner-city gardens often stay warmer because of heat emitted from surrounding buildings and walls.
- Gardens located near large bodies of water (such as lochs and the sea) are protected from the extremes of temperature.

Weather facts

- Northern and western areas of the UK experience the strongest gales.
- Eastern parts of the UK receive more sunshine than those in the west.
- The central Highlands of Scotland is the coldest area of the UK, and the southern tip of Cornwall is the warmest.
- It is officially summer when the temperature rises above 18°C. Summers in the south of the UK can be twice as long as those in the north.

The Royal Botanic Garden Edinburgh consists of four Gardens: our Edinburgh Garden, Benmore in Argyll, Dawyck in the Scottish Borders and Logan in Galloway. The different climates experienced at these four sites is a good illustration of the variation that occurs across the country. Here are some examples across a 7-year gap to show how different conditions can be.

	Maximum Temperature (°C)		Minimum Temperature (°C)		Last frost		First frost		Annual precipitation (mm)	
	2018	2011	2018	2011	2018	2011	2018	2011	2018	2011
Edinburgh	27.8	24.9	-6.1	-6.4	18 May	10 June	23 Sept	20 Oct	897.4	843.1
Benmore	30.9	24.6	-6.4	-6.3	1 May	11 June	16 Oct	18 Oct	2403.3	3,360.2
Dawyck	29.3	24.8	-9.3	-11.0	1 May	10 June	23 Sept	19 Oct	923.0	1,253.7
Logan	22.5	22.0	-5.0	-3.6	29 April	29 Mar	9 Nov	6 Nov	858.4	710.8

Tips for successful growing

- Observe neighbours' gardens, local allotments and public gardens to see what is growing. Find out about your area from local gardening groups or allotment holders.

- Experienced gardeners will be able to tell you about characteristics such as weather and soil type.

- Listen to and watch weather forecasts to gain early warnings of high winds or extremes in temperature.

- Keep a garden notebook to record the weather and your crop successes and failures for future reference.

- Learn to work with the weather and your particular garden conditions. Every year will be different, but that's the challenge and the fun of growing your own.

Growing in Scotland

We can grow some fantastic vegetables in Scotland. With careful planning and innovative techniques it is possible to grow some crops all year round. The main challenge is the climate: we have a shorter growing season to work in. Spring arrives later and autumn arrives earlier than further south. Don't be put off because there is nothing more rewarding than sitting down and eating your own produce. Talk to your neighbours and find out which varieties grow well in your region. But don't be afraid to experiment and try at least one new thing each year.

Making the most of space

Even the smallest space can yield a crop. Edible plants can be grown on windowsills, balconies, small gardens or on your doorstep.

Container gardens

If you have space for containers you can grow many different vegetables successfully. You can use anything from traditional pots and window boxes to yoghurt pots, paint tins and old welly boots, so long as they have holes in the bottom. Choose containers large enough to accommodate the eventual size of your plant and consider the material they are made of. More porous pots like terracotta and wooden containers will dry out quickly.

Things to consider

Give a thought to aesthetics. Grow things that look good, such as runner beans, rainbow chard and the uncommon 'Golden Sweet' yellow-podded mange-tout pea, which also has pretty purple flowers. You could grow some ornamental plants with edible flowers such as nasturtiums, calendula and borage.

Watch out for pests: the vine weevil is very fond of container-grown plants, and slugs and snails congregate around the base of pots. Containers are vulnerable to frost so you need to protect them in winter.

Wrap pots in horticultural fleece or bubble wrap and move them to a sheltered position, grouping them together to provide extra shelter. During winter do not let pots stand sodden; remove trays from underneath them and raise them up from the ground.

Choosing a container

Smaller containers
(20cm diameter)
Perfect for compact crops,
such as herbs and salads

Larger pots
(45cm diameter)
For more vigorous plants,
such as potatoes,
tomatoes, courgettes

Deep pots
(25cm-deep minimum)
Necessary for root crops and beans

Compost – Use multipurpose compost. Organic and peat-free is best for the environment. Use fresh compost each time you plant up.

Feeding and watering – Add water-retaining granules to the compost and water regularly as pots can dry out very quickly. You will need to feed your pots, as plants soon use up the nutrients in the compost. Liquid feed is best added once a fortnight, whilst slow-release fertilisers should be applied at the start of the growing season. There are a range of organic options available.

Good crops to try

- Beetroot
- Carrots – 'Early Nantes' is quick-growing
- Courgettes and squashes
- Dwarf French beans
- Herbs
- Potatoes – they grow happily in large pots or even old compost bags with holes
- Salad – baby-leaf varieties can be picked continuously

Look out for baby vegetables and varieties marked as 'dwarf', 'patio' or 'container' plants. Crops with a good ratio of harvest to space are best. For example, a successful courgette plant will provide several kilograms of fruit in the same space it takes to grow just a few onions.

Vertical gardens

You can use height in your garden to make the most of space. Here are some ideas:

- Use a hanging basket to grow herbs or tomatoes.
- Use a trellis for climbers such as beans and peas, or sprawling plants such as cucumbers and squash (tie these in well and prop up their fruits).
- Put plants on shelves or fix pots directly onto the wall.
- A range of purpose-built vertical growing systems can be purchased online or at garden centres.

It is best not to position containers too high as they will be difficult to water and harvest. Choose your wall position carefully: south-facing is best for warm, sheltered growing conditions, but other positions can be used too provided they receive sufficient sunlight.

Good crops to try

- Loose-leaf lettuces
- Cut-and-come-again salads, such as rocket
- Herbs such as basil, parsley, coriander, sage, thyme, rosemary and oregano
- Tomatoes – 'Tumbling Tom' is ideal for hanging baskets
- Climbing plants such as climbing cucumbers, French beans, runner beans, squash 'Tromboncino'

Planning the space in your plots

Even in a small outdoor space a colourful and productive plot can supply vegetables and flowers for most of the year. You can achieve this by having a designated vegetable area (raised beds or garden bed) or by mixing vegetables with your existing flower borders to create a decorative but edible display.

There are various approaches to utilising your outside growing space.

▼ **Flat beds** – where the soil level is flush with the surrounding land. Often used where lawn has been lifted to produce a square or rectangular plot. These are used at the Royal Botanic Garden Edinburgh (RBGE).

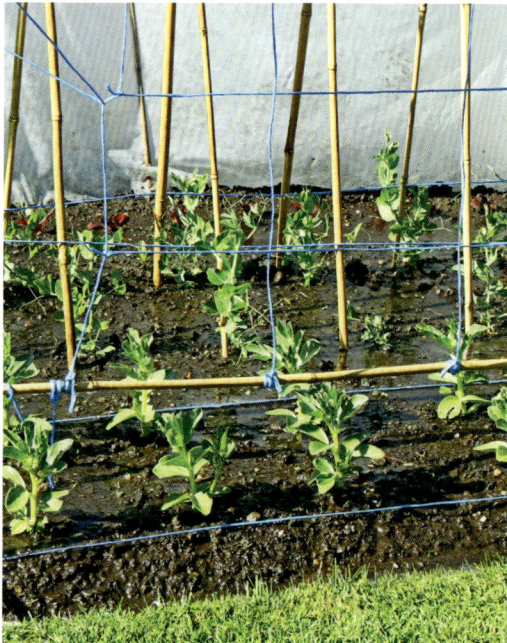

▼ **Mixed border** – where you utilise your existing borders to incorporate edible plants, making them both decorative and functional. This can be informal, with the odd vegetable (kale, lettuce), or a full-scale potager.

▼ **Raised beds** – where the soil is contained by wood or brick edging. This method provides good drainage, allowing the soil to warm quickly early in the season and reduce bending when cultivating. It can also help to overcome problems such as low or high pH, as you can add appropriate soil into raised areas.

Considerations

Other things to consider:

- Permanent stepping stones or paths allow you to have access to the plants without standing on the soil.

- Narrow beds are best because plants can be reached easily from either side.

- Consider access to other facilities like watering point, tools and composting, to avoid long trips back and forth.

- Try to avoid overhanging trees, hedges and shrubs that can compete for moisture and light.

- Avoid shading of other plants by placing short plants in front of tall crops to maximise sunlight.

RBGE's first-year HND/BSc Horticulture with Plantsmanship students each take responsibility for a small plot (2 × 6.5m) in the Garden. Each student must grow five vegetables (broad beans, peas, beetroot, lettuce and onions) at one end of their plot and the remaining area can be grown with any fruit, flowers or vegetables they choose. This layout is reversed each year to help avoid soil-borne pests and diseases. The students develop their horticultural skills: planning; soil preparation; crop selection; sowing; and on-going plant maintenance including watering, feeding, supporting and protecting crops, and come up with creative designs and solutions to growing in a small space.

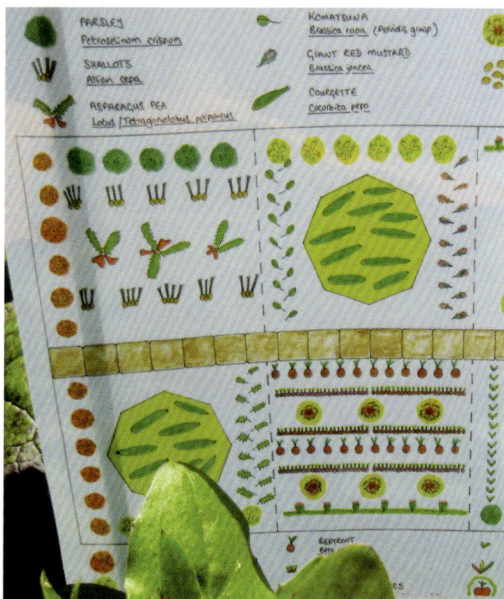

Our student plots

Many students give their plots a theme in order to help narrow down their plant options. Previous students have used the following themes:

- Colour – purples and greens; strawberries and cream; black and white
- Traditional vegetable garden – ornamental potager; edible flowers; heritage seeds
- Particular countries or foods – the Auld Alliance (French and Scottish plants); baby vegetables; Japanese/oriental crops; growing a three-course menu
- Medicinal plants
- Techniques – biodynamic growing; companion planting; sustainable growing; square foot gardening

To fit with the academic year the plot assessment runs from October to May, so the students have the additional challenge of bringing forward their crops and flowers for a very early deadline.

Many of the students have never grown anything before so the plot gives them the opportunity to have a go and exchange ideas with each other, RBGE horticultural staff, volunteers and the visiting public. Often the best ideas come through collaboration.

Some of the RBGE students' ideas

- Instant raised beds, using reclaimed drawers with the bottoms knocked out
- Raised strawberry bed to avoid slugs and utilise space below with shade-tolerant crops
- Structures to support climbing plants that also serve as a barrier
- Introducing small ponds to encourage wildlife and beneficial predators
- Creating a hot bed using old tyres and a cloche cover to grow courgettes
- Using insectivorous plants to control aphids

Gardening in difficult conditions

Your garden, or some areas of it, might not offer the optimum conditions for vegetable growing; however most challenges can be overcome.

Heavy clay soils

Clay soils can be tricky for growing as the soil takes longer to warm up in the spring, is slower to drain and is prone to compaction, which makes it harder to work. This results in plant roots being unable to penetrate through the soil. Heavy soils are very fertile and the drainage and soil structure can be improved over time.

Improve soil structure

- By adding organic matter (see p. 38).
- By applying calcium in the form of lime on acid soils or gypsum on alkaline soils to encourage the clay to break down into crumbs.

Raised beds

Build raised beds and fill them with good imported soil. These beds help prevent the earth becoming compacted as they can be worked without standing on the soil. They can be filled with top soil or covered with a layer of organic matter (no-dig method; see p. 39) to improve the soil structure over time.

Crops to grow

Crops that grow on heavy soils include:

- Brassicas (cabbages, broccoli, cauliflowers), which prefer the firm and nutrient-rich soils.
- Potatoes can help to break up the soil. The addition of organic matter when they are 'earthed up' will also improve the soil structure and drainage over time.
- Runner, French and broad beans that have vigorous roots should grow well.

Tips

- Start off all vegetables in containers and then transplant them into their final position.
- Avoid root crops (carrots, parsnips, beetroots) that will struggle to push through the clay soil. Grow them in large pots instead!

Shade-tolerant plants

Most vegetables develop larger yields when grown in full sunshine, but many produce a decent harvest in a shady position. Shady spots are cooler, darker and often drier, which slows down plant growth. Some crops are more tolerant than others and will continue to produce with just a few hours of sunshine a day.

Crops to grow

Deep shade (two to three hours' sunlight):

- Chervil, lettuce and salad leaf crops (American land cress, mizuna, pak choi, rocket, spinach, winter purslane), parsley, sorrel and wild garlic

Partial shade (three to four hours' sunlight):

- All the above crops plus beetroot, chard, chicory, chives, coriander, kale, mint, radish, rhubarb, turnip and wild strawberries

Also consider

- Early-maturing peas ('Kelvedon Wonder'), broad beans and plants that grow towards the light (climbing beans, Jerusalem artichokes)
- Unusual or hedgerow crops such as Alexanders, Good King Henry, hedge mustard, Solomon's seal and sweet cicely

Tips

- Thin out branches on nearby trees to maximise light.
- Paint shady walls a light colour to reflect available light.

Exposed sites

Winds can devastate crops through drying them out and knocking them to the ground. Coastal gardens tend to be milder than inland sites, but salt spray can seriously damage crops. Crops grown on balconies or in window boxes can also suffer in windy conditions. The best solution is to provide shelter and to grow plants adapted to these conditions.

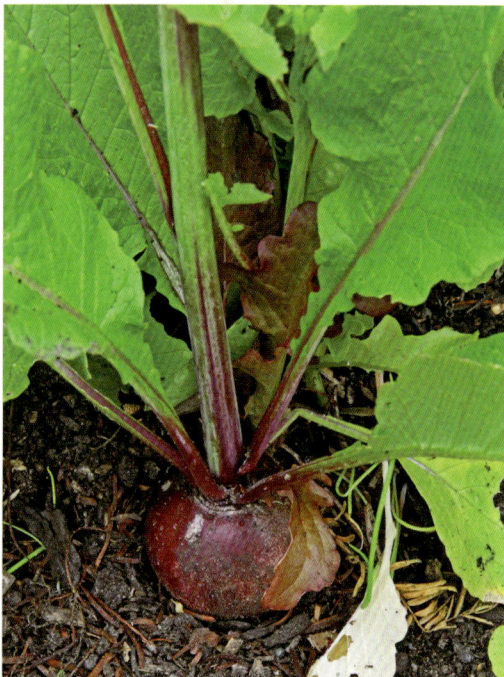

Shelter

- Grow a shelter belt using wind- and/or salt-tolerant trees and shrubs (escallonia, euonymus, fuchsia, hawthorn, juniper, Scots pine, sea buckthorn).
- Build a semi-permeable wall or fence to shelter crops.
- Purchase a polytunnel, greenhouse or other form of protected environment.

Crops to grow

Wind-tolerant plants:

- Root vegetables (beetroots, carrots, garlic, horseradish – bear in mind horseradish can be very invasive – onions and parsnips)
- Low-growing herbs (rosemary, thyme)
- Plants adapted to coastal sites: chard, fennel, lovage, samphire, sea beet and sea kale

Growing at height

If growing on an exposed balcony:

- Secure containers properly.
- Use water-retaining granules in the compost.
- Avoid using porous pots that dry out quickly.
- Grow robust, wind-resistant herbs (chives, marjoram, oregano, parsley, rosemary and thyme).

Pot garden ideas

If you only have a patio, balcony, windowsill or front steps there are still lots of crops you can grow successfully in pots. Be inventive and choose crops you will use and which look nice. You can theme your plants, for example by colour, country or a food dish. Here are some ideas.

Outdoor summer pots

Soup pot

Ingredients to make a tasty pot of soup – in addition, the onions may help to deter carrot root fly.

- Carrots ('Flyaway', 'Purple Haze')
- Coriander
- Onions ('Long Red Florence') or spring onions ('Performer')

Summer salad pot

Interesting textures, colours and flavours for a summer salad.

- Lettuce ('Dazzle')
- Mustard ('Red Frills')
- Nasturtium ('Princess of India' – edible flowers and leaves)
- Rocket

Colour-themed crops

These add a splash of colour to make your crops both edible and decorative.

Purple

- Dwarf French bean ('Purple Queen')
- Mustard ('Red Frills')
- Purple basil ('Dark Opal')

Red

- Broad beans ('Crimson Flowered')
- Lettuce ('Lollo Rosso')
- Red orach

Sunny herb pot

For adding flavour to salads, stews and soups.

- Chives
- Rosemary
- Thyme

Shade-tolerant pot

Ideal for areas without direct sunlight.

- Coriander
- Spinach ('Winter Giant', 'Reddy')
- Swiss chard ('Ruby Red')

Indoor summer pots

Grown in individual pots

- Aubergines
- Cucumbers
- Melons
- Peppers
- Tomatoes

Outdoor winter pots

Winter greens

- Kale ('Nero di Toscano', 'Russian Red')
- Lamb's lettuce
- Pak choi

Indoor winter pots

Winter salad

- Lettuce ('Winter Density', 'Valdor')
- Parsley
- Radicchio ('Di Treviso')

Windowsill pots

Grown in individual pots

- Chillies
- Chives
- Mint
- Pea shoots

Plant crops requiring similar conditions in the same pot (for example sun-loving, shade-tolerant, deep- or shallow-rooting, hungry feeders). If the plants you want to grow are not compatible then grow them separately. Often groups of three different-sized pots look good positioned together. Also, think about how the contrasting colours or textures will look.

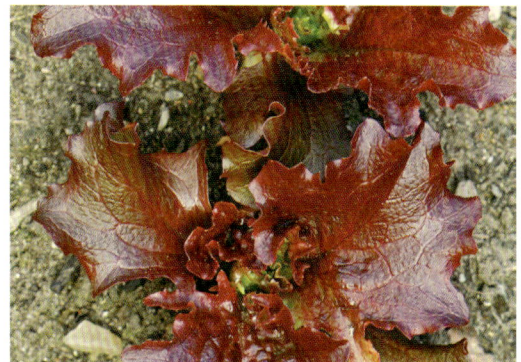

Crop rotation

All crops have different soil requirements and planting certain vegetables in the same beds year after year can lead to problems. Altering where you grow crops in your plot reduces the chance of soil nutrient deficiencies developing or crop-specific pests persisting.

The grouping and rotating of crops also allows you to make soil treatments more targeted and crop-specific. For example, nutrient-rich manure or compost can be applied before heavy feeding crops are planted but avoided where unnecessary. Lime can be added to reduce soil acidity, which helps avoid clubroot in cabbages; however, this is bad for potatoes as it can encourage scab.

A systematic rotation can also be helpful in weed control. Crops such as potatoes and courgettes have dense foliage which suppresses weeds, continuing to reduce problems in following crops. Growing these before crops with sparser foliage, such as carrots and onions, makes them less likely to suffer competition from weeds.

Grouping vegetables

Vegetables are grouped by their plant families, because vegetables within the same families tend to have the same soil requirements and same pest and disease risks. Below is one example of how the families can be organised into four groups within similar requirements.

Potato (Solanaceae):
potatoes

Brassicas (Brassicaceae):
Brussels sprouts, cabbages, cauliflowers, kale, kohl-rabi, oriental greens, radishes, swedes, turnips

Beets (Chenopodiaceae):
beetroot, chard, spinach
Carrots (Apiaceae):
carrots, celeriac, celery, fennel, parsley
Onions (Alliaceae):
garlic, leeks, onions, shallots

Legumes (Fabaceae or Leguminosae):
broad beans, French and runner beans, peas

Salads (including chicory, endives and lettuce) and sweetcorn, plus cucurbits (Cucurbitaceae) such as courgettes, cucumbers, marrows, pumpkins and squashes, can be grown wherever convenient, but avoid growing them too often in the same place.

Perennials such as artichokes, asparagus and rhubarb do not fit into the rotation; these should be established in their own beds and not rotated.

Limitations

While crop rotations can be extremely helpful there are limits. They should be seen as helping to control pests and disease rather than a complete cure. Depending on space, your plots may be quite close to one another, so pests can still spread to other crops. Additionally, some diseases can stay in the soil for a long time; clubroot and white onion rot, for example, can persist in the soil for up to 20 years, making rotations impractically long.

The groups can be difficult to organise as they require different amounts of space; for example, a large proportion of crops are brassicas. Some crops such as parsnips stay in the ground for extended periods, disrupting the rotation. We recommend a flexible approach to the idea of rotation. Keep records to help plan future cropping.

A sample crop rotation

The main groupings can be grown together and organised in a number of ways. This diagram shows two sample plans:

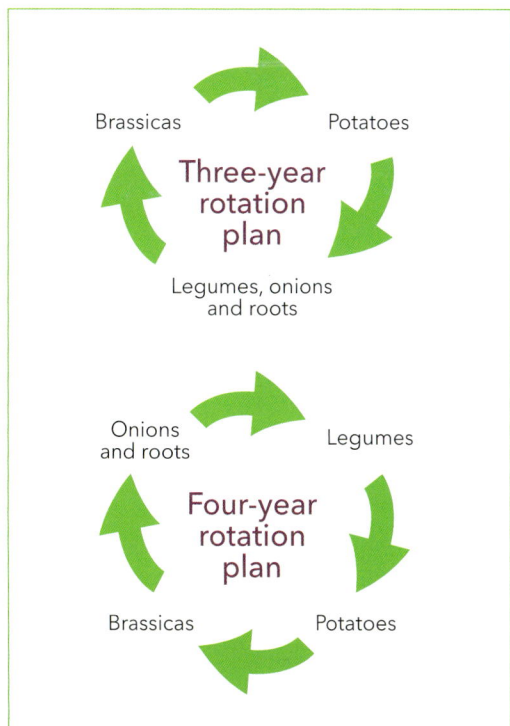

Brassicas   Potatoes

Three-year rotation plan

Legumes, onions and roots

Onions and roots   Legumes

Four-year rotation plan

Brassicas   Potatoes

Planning for continuity

One of the great skills of vegetable growing is to keep the ground in year-round harvest, providing continuous harvests while overcoming a sequence of gluts and famines. If you are well organised, summer crops can be followed by winter crops. These will need to be started in seed trays or pots ready for immediate planting out after the previous crop. Vegetables such as purple sprouting broccoli and spring greens are ready to harvest early in the season, while parsnips, leeks and swedes can be harvested all through the winter.

Winter crops

Winter vegetables require more forethought and planning as fewer crops grow during the coldest months. Although growth comes to a virtual standstill because of low light and temperatures, there are crops that are relatively winter hardy and can continue to provide fresh harvests. All of these crops will benefit from some protection, especially in a severe winter.

Winter crops include:

- Brassicas, for example Brussels sprouts, cabbages, kale, purple sprouting broccoli and swedes
- Celeriac
- Herbs, for example chervil, coriander, parsley, rosemary and thyme
- Rainbow chard and spinach
- Leeks
- Parsnips
- Winter salads, for example corn salad (lamb's lettuce), land cress and winter purslane

Brassicas, celeriac, leeks and parsnips grow slowly. They need to be sown early in the season to ensure they have reached a decent size by the time growth stops. Celeriac and parsnips may need sowing as early as March. Winter salads need sowing in late summer to ensure they are big enough to survive but have not matured too far.

The 'hungry gap'

The months of April, May and June are known as the 'hungry gap' because they are the most difficult time for harvesting. Winter and stored vegetables are coming to an end (or spoiling) and the crops from spring sowings have not yet reached maturity.

Vegetables available during the hungry gap:

- Winter vegetables such as purple sprouting broccoli (the flowering stems of any brassicas can be eaten when young and tender), leaf beet, leeks and spinach.

- Overwintering plants like spring cabbages, spring cauliflower and nine-star perennial broccoli.

- New growth from perennials such as asparagus, chives, rhubarb and sorrel.

- Fast-growing vegetables sown in April and protected with cloches, for example beetroot, lettuce, pea shoots, radish, rocket and spinach.

- The first tender broad beans may be available by the beginning of June.

- Wild harvests – supplement cultivated crops with fresh growth from wild plants such as dandelions, fat-hen, nettles and wild garlic. These may be weeds on your plot!

Value-for-space

When planning for continuity it is worth assessing the 'value-for-space' of crops.

- Plants like pumpkin, squashes and sweetcorn that take up a lot of space for a relatively small reward may not be best for a small garden.

- Space-saving cultivars mean more crops from limited space; small cultivars are available of aubergines, courgettes, peas, peppers and tomatoes.

- Some plants, such as leeks and parsnips, can be harvested over a long period of time, giving good value.

Some crops take up a lot of space and are cheap in the shops so it may be better to grow choice crops that are expensive or difficult to buy.

Length of time to reach maturity

- **Slow-growing crops** – aubergines, Brussels sprouts, cabbages, celeriac, maincrop carrots, garlic, salsify, swede and sweet peppers.

- **Quick-growing crops** – beetroot, early carrots, dwarf French beans, pak choi, early peas, early potatoes, radish, rocket, summer lettuce and turnips, as well as Asian greens such as choy sum, mibuna, mizuna and mustard leaf.

Multiple harvests from individual plants

Cut-and-come again and baby-leaf salads, such as leaf beet, loose-leaved lettuces, rocket and spinach will regrow after they are first cut. Once leaves have reached a useable size, cut all but the central rosette of young leaves, which will regrow. This can provide up to three harvests.

- For some crops, such as chard, kale, oriental greens and salad bowl lettuce, it is possible to pick older leaves as they become large enough; this encourages new ones to develop.

- Mature cut-and-come again – once mature heads of several crops have been harvested the remaining stumps can be left to resprout, for example spring and summer cabbages, overwintering lettuce, Chinese cabbage and pak choi.

- Florence fennel and beetroot can provide a small quantity of leaves as well as roots; don't remove too many leaves, however, or the roots will not develop.

Selecting varieties for year-round supply

Look for:

- Early croppers – varieties that take less time to reach a harvestable age
- Those that mature in different seasons

Vegetables with varieties that crop at different times of the year:

- Potatoes
  - First earlies: plant late March/April, protect from frost, harvest June
  - Second earlies: plant late March/April, protect from frost, harvest July/August
  - Maincrop: plant mid-April/May, harvest September/October
  - 'Christmas potatoes': it is possible to plant cold-stored early potatoes (available from specialist suppliers) in August. Protected from early frosts these will provide a late harvest of new potatoes in time for Christmas.
- Brussels sprouts – varieties crop from August to March
- Cabbages
- Calabrese – varieties crop from July to September
- Carrots
- Cauliflower
- Leeks – varieties crop from August to March
- Asian greens, for example pak choi, mizuna and mibuna
- Peas – varieties crop from May to October
- Salad leaves/lettuce
- Spring onions
- Sprouting broccoli

When purchasing seed try to share packets with friends or neighbours. For example buy one packet of cauliflower seeds each but get both winter-cropping and summer-cropping varieties and share the seeds out; this will improve the continuity of supply for the same cost.

Intercropping

Quick-growing vegetables can be sown in between slower-growing large crops, such as brassicas, to provide an early harvest. You can also grow shade-tolerant crops such as spinach and land cress between rows of tall crops such as runner beans (undercropping). This can help to confuse crop-specific pests and limit weeds, because less bare soil is available for weed germination. Quick crops can act as markers for those slower to germinate, for example radishes sown with parsnips.

Quick-growing or small crops suitable for intercropping:

- Corn salad
- Cut-and-come-again salad leaves
- Early carrots
- Lettuce
- Miniature pak choi
- Radish
- Spinach
- Spring onions

Slow-growing crops suitable for intercropping:

- Cauliflowers, broccoli, Brussels sprouts
- Celeriac
- Parsnips
- Salsify

Tall/climbing plants suitable for undercropping:

- Beans
- Squashes and cucumber (if trained up supports)
- Sweetcorn

Catch cropping/ Double cropping

A quick-growing crop can be planted before or after the main slower-growing crop; any of the quick crops listed for intercropping may be used. Green manures are also suitable for a catch crop (see p. 40). Examples of suitable crop plans include:

- Spring greens sown July/August, harvested March > radishes sown March, harvested May/June > tender summer crops, for example runner beans
- Broad beans sown March/April, harvested June/July > Oriental leaves sown July, harvested October (or overwinter if given protection)
- Lettuce sown late March, harvested late May/ June > courgettes or squashes planted out
- Onions planted March, harvested August/ September > sow green manure August/ September, mustard or *Phacelia* dug in late October/November

Successional sowing

This is a system of sowing the same crop at intervals of time, so the plants reach harvest at different points. It helps to prevent gluts and is especially useful for crops that have to be harvested soon after maturity and don't store well. Sow again after the first crop is well established, that is with four 'true' leaves above ground. Fluctuating environmental conditions can lead to varying germination and establishment rates. It is often beneficial to make two sowings of crops such as courgettes, runner beans and early potatoes (see 'Christmas potatoes' p. 25) to prolong the harvest period.

Quick-growing crops suitable for successional sowing include:

- Beetroot
- Early peas
- Kohl-rabi
- Radish
- Spinach
- Early carrots
- French beans
- Lettuce
- Rocket
- Spring onions

Storage

To help provide a continuous supply be sure to grow vegetables that can be stored and familiarise yourself with a range of storage techniques (see p. 66).

Forced vegetables

Some vegetables can be 'forced' into producing an earlier crop, a common practice with Victorian gardeners.

- Rhubarb – in winter cover dormant buds with straw or leaves and place a large light-excluding container on top. Tender pink stems will be produced a few weeks later.

- Chicory – lift roots in early winter, pot up and exclude light. A blanched cluster of tender leaves (chicon) will be produced three to four weeks later.

Hot beds

Cover a 60–90cm layer of fresh manure with 20–30cm of soil/compost. The manure warms the soil as it decomposes, leading to better conditions for crops. This can be used to speed up seedling growth or protect tender crops, extending the harvest. Using hot beds in conjunction with protection will give the best results.

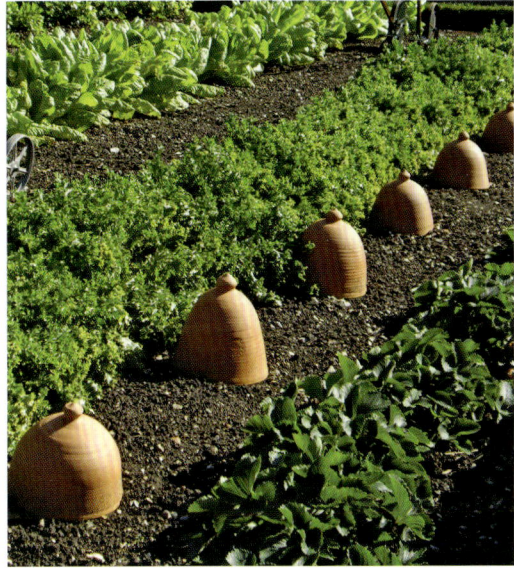

Extending the growing season using protection

If plants are sheltered from cold conditions they will continue to grow for longer. Try any of these:

- Windowsill
- Heated propagator
- Polytunnel
- Greenhouse
- Cold frame
- Cloches

To make the best use of cloches, group together plants that will be sown and harvested at the same time, for example all overwintering vegetables together, all tender vegetables together and so on.

Crops that can be grown on your windowsill all year round:

- Herbs (coriander, chervil, parsley)
- Micro salads
- Pea shoots
- Specially selected salad mixes
- Sprouting seeds

Sample plot plan

Small garden

Key considerations

- Think about the aesthetics of your vegetable garden and choose attractive cultivars/varieties.
- Vegetables can be mixed with ornamentals.
- Crop rotation may be difficult so don't worry about it too much; just try not to plant the same thing in the same place year after year.
- In a small garden it is more likely that you will have to grow some of your vegetables in non-optimum conditions, such as shade, because you have less choice in where you can grow them. Choose crops that will cope best with any tricky situations (see p. 14).
- Double cropping is even more valuable – look for early-maturing varieties such as radish and those that provide long harvest periods such as mange-tout peas.
- Save space by avoiding bulky crops that are cheap to buy in the shops, such as potatoes.
- Leave room to sit, relax and enjoy the fruits of your labour.

Plan for vegetables in a small front garden

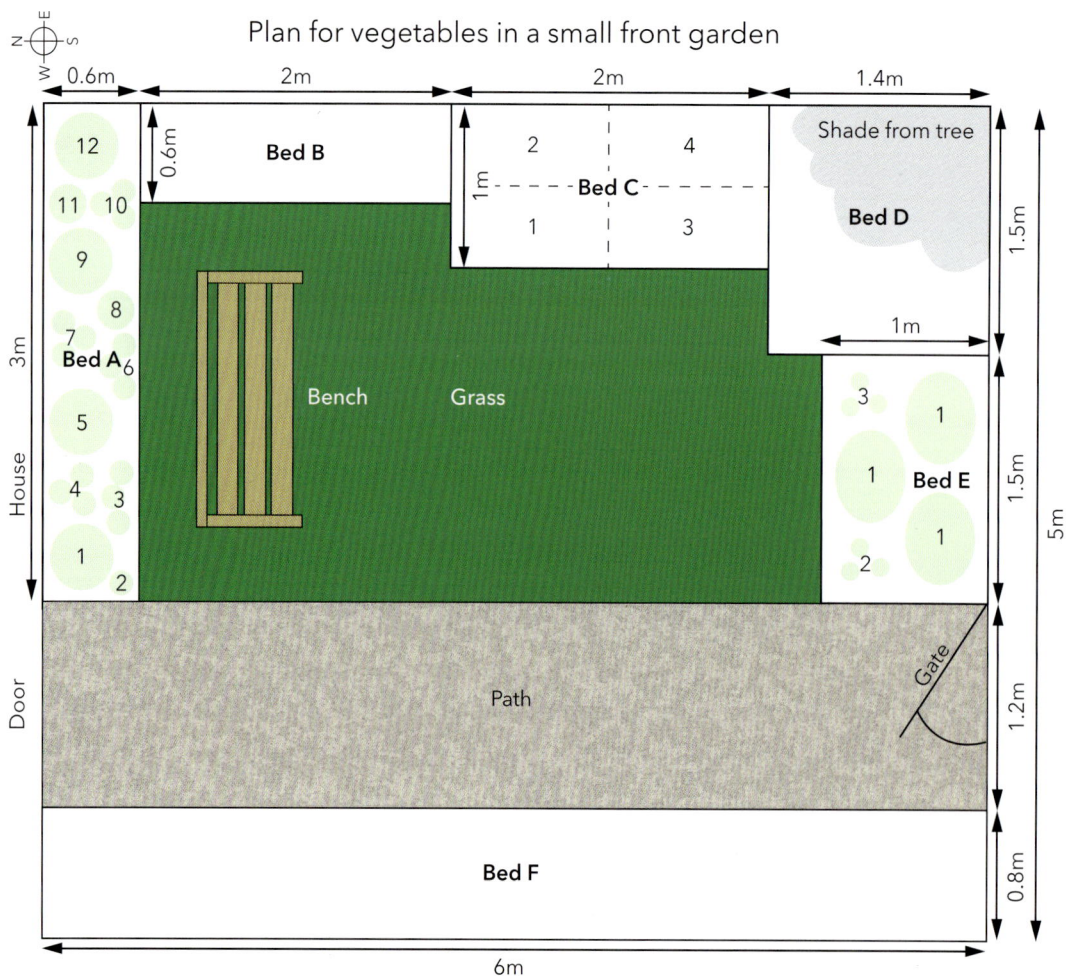

Bed A (Dimensions: 3 × 0.6m)

Culinary herbs
Mix or perennials to provide year-round structure and annuals:

1 Rosemary 'Miss Jessopp's Upright'
2 Creeping thyme
3 Chives (×3)
4 Flat-leaf parsley
5 Sage
6 Garlic chives
7 Coriander (spring/autumn, may over winter with protection) Basil (×3) (summer)
8 Thyme
9 Fennel
10 Chervil
11 Marjoram
12 Bay

Bed B (Dimensions: 0.6 × 2m)

Cut-and-come-again salads
Ready prepared mixes are available. Include varieties with decorative leaves:

- Lettuce 'Cocarde'
- Lettuce 'Green Oak Leaf'
- Mizuna
- Mustard 'Golden Streaks'
- Mustard 'Red Frills'
- Salad rocket

Bed C (Dimensions: 1 × 2m)

1 Carrots, for example 'Nantes 2' – early variety sow in March and May, approximately 18 plants (15cm spread per plant)
2 Beetroot, for example 'Boltardy' – grow as 'baby' beetroot, i.e. rows 7cm apart, 6cm between individual plants; sow in March and May
3 Rainbow chard, approximately five plants
4 Dwarf French beans, for example 'Purple Queen' (purple podded), ten plants

Bed D (Dimensions: 1.5 × 1.4m)

Shady bed
Leafy crops such as:

- Kale 'Cavolo Nero' for winter use
- Lettuce 'Salad Bowl'
- Mint, for example garden mint (for cooking) and peppermint (for tea); plant in large pots sunk into the ground to prevent the roots spreading
- Spinach

Bed E (Dimensions: 1.5 × 1m)

1 Courgettes 'Buckingham' F1 (compact plant, yellow-skinned) (×3)
2 Nasturtiums 'Tom Thumb'
3 Pot marigolds

Bed F (Dimensions: 0.8 × 6m)

Long narrow beds are suitable for climbing plants as long as sufficient supports are provided:

- Runner beans 'Polestar' (red flowers)
- Peas
- Cordon tomatoes 'Gardener's Delight'
- Sweet peas

Annual flowers such as French marigolds or small crops such as spring onions, radishes and salad leaves can be planted as a catch crop along the path edge.

Large garden

General considerations

- In a large garden an area can be laid out specifically for vegetables.
- Choose an area that is in full sun and well sheltered.

'Companion plants'

A range of flowers can be included to attract beneficial insects. These plants will also make the plot look more attractive. Examples include:

- French marigolds
- Sweet peas
- Poached-egg plant
- Edible flowers such as nasturtiums, pot marigold, sunflowers and borage

Large garden sample plot plan (summer)

Bed width = 1.2m ideal for reaching into the centre of the bed without having to tread on it

Path width 0.6-0.9m to allow space for wheelbarrow, kneeling for weeding

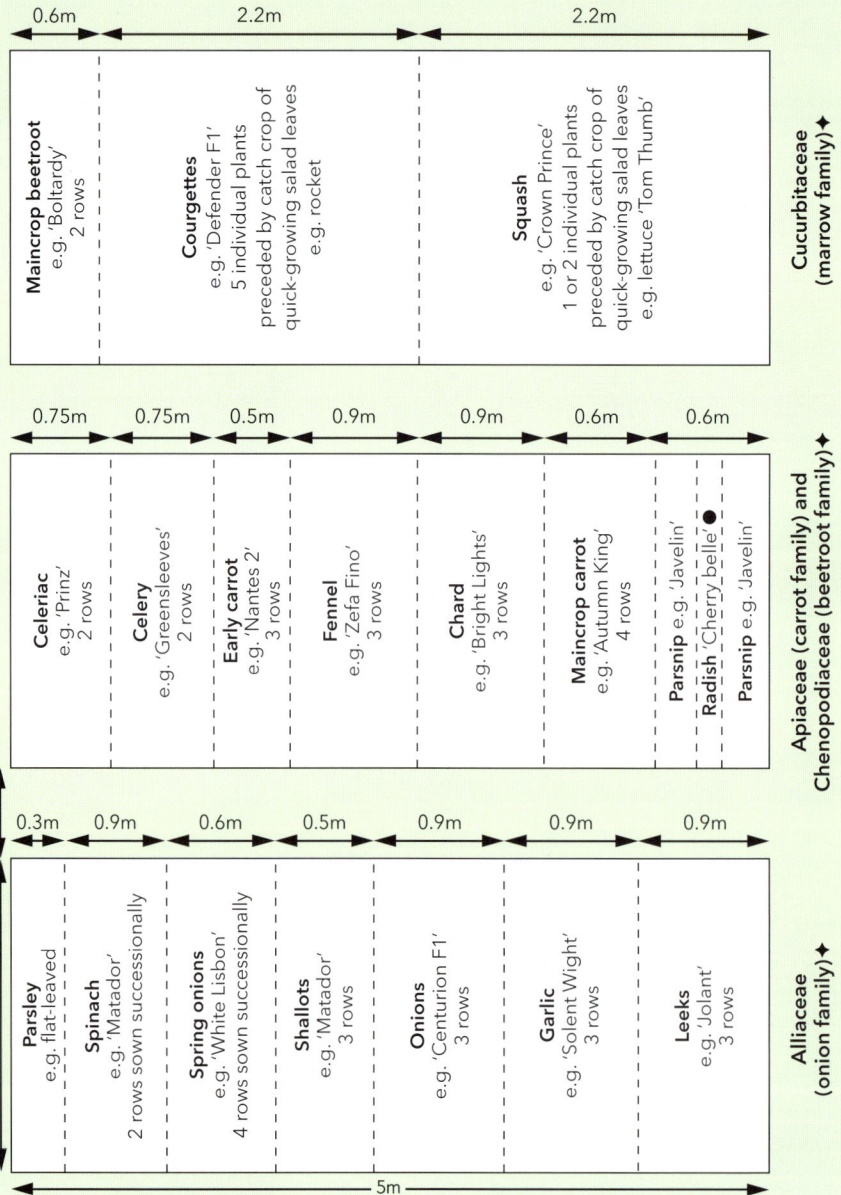

Cucurbitaceae (marrow family) ✦

0.6m	2.2m	2.2m
Maincrop beetroot e.g. 'Boltardy' 2 rows	**Courgettes** e.g. 'Defender F1' 5 individual plants preceded by catch crop of quick-growing salad leaves e.g. rocket	**Squash** e.g. 'Crown Prince' 1 or 2 individual plants preceded by catch crop of quick-growing salad leaves e.g. lettuce 'Tom Thumb'

Apiaceae (carrot family) and Chenopodiaceae (beetroot family) ✦

0.75m	0.75m	0.5m	0.9m	0.9m	0.6m	0.6m
Celeriac e.g. 'Prinz' 2 rows	**Celery** e.g. 'Greensleeves' 2 rows	**Early carrot** e.g. 'Nantes 2' 3 rows	**Fennel** e.g. 'Zefa Fino' 3 rows	**Chard** e.g. 'Bright Lights' 3 rows	**Maincrop carrot** e.g. 'Autumn King' 4 rows	**Parsnip** e.g. 'Javelin' **Radish** 'Cherry belle' ● **Parsnip** e.g. 'Javelin'

Alliaceae (onion family) ✦

0.3m	0.9m	0.6m	0.5m	0.9m	0.9m	0.9m
Parsley e.g. flat-leaved	**Spinach** e.g. 'Matador' 2 rows sown successionally	**Spring onions** e.g. 'White Lisbon' 4 rows sown successionally	**Shallots** e.g. 'Matador' 3 rows	**Onions** e.g. 'Centurion F1' 3 rows	**Garlic** e.g. 'Solent Wight' 3 rows	**Leeks** e.g. 'Jolant' 3 rows

5m

Double cropping

Where possible attempt to double crop each bed. Crops that are planted out late, such as squashes, can be preceded by quick-growing crops such as loose-leaved salads or radishes. Early-finishing crops can be followed by winter crops, quick-growing crops or green manures, for example early carrots followed by overwintering leeks.

Crop rotation

The following year rotate the plots anti-clockwise: alliums followed by legumes; legumes followed by potatoes; potatoes followed by brassicas and so on.

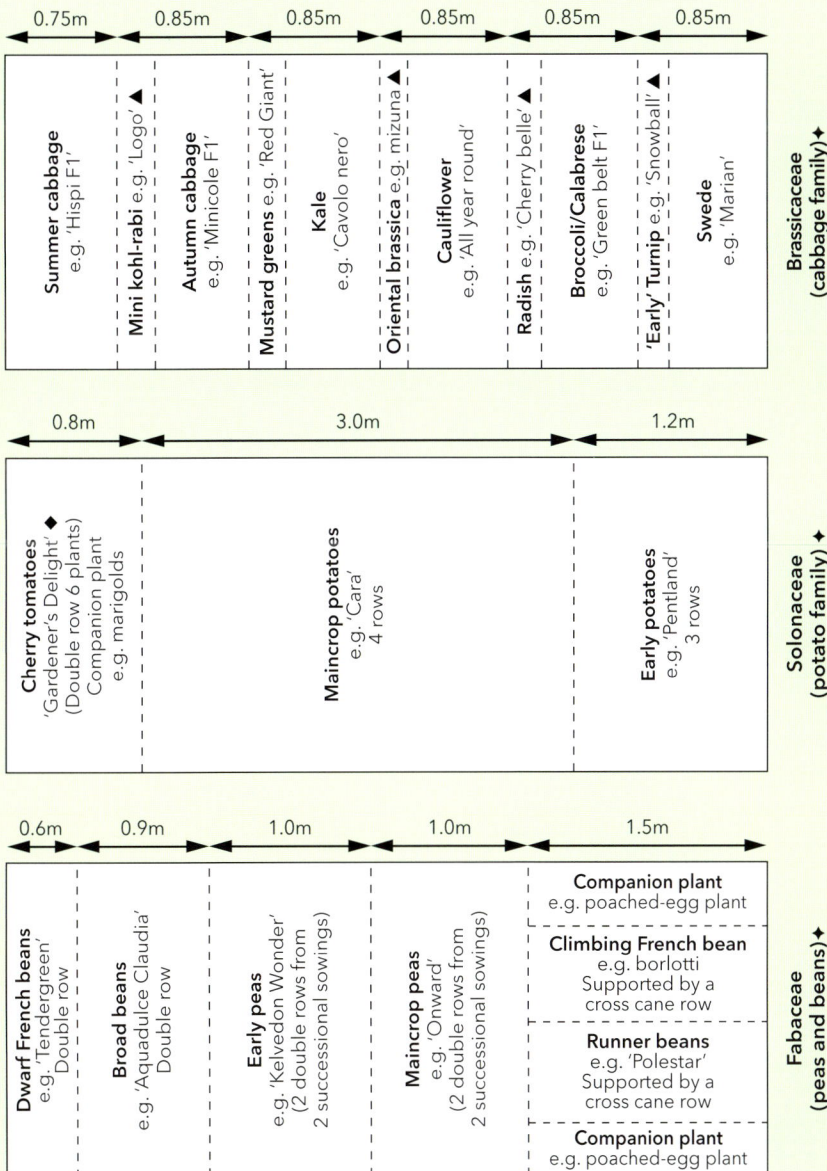

0.75m   0.85m   0.85m   0.85m   0.85m   0.85m

| Summer cabbage e.g. 'Hispi F1' | Mini kohl-rabi e.g. 'Logo' ◀ | Autumn cabbage e.g. 'Minicole F1' | Mustard greens e.g. 'Red Giant' | Kale e.g. 'Cavolo nero' | Oriental brassica e.g. mizuna ◀ | Cauliflower e.g. 'All year round' | Radish e.g. 'Cherry belle' ◀ | Broccoli/Calabrese e.g. 'Green belt F1' | 'Early' Turnip e.g. 'Snowball' ◀ | Swede e.g. 'Marian' |

Brassicaceae (cabbage family) ✦

0.8m   3.0m   1.2m

| Cherry tomatoes 'Gardener's Delight' ◆ (Double row 6 plants) Companion plant e.g. marigolds | Maincrop potatoes e.g. 'Cara' 4 rows | Early potatoes e.g. 'Pentland' 3 rows |

Solonaceae (potato family) ✦

0.6m   0.9m   1.0m   1.0m   1.5m

| Dwarf French beans e.g. 'Tendergreen' Double row | Broad beans e.g. 'Aquadulce Claudia' Double row | Early peas e.g. 'Kelvedon Wonder' (2 double rows from 2 successional sowings) | Maincrop peas e.g. 'Onward' (2 double rows from 2 successional sowings) | Companion plant e.g. poached-egg plant
Climbing French bean e.g. borlotti Supported by a cross cane row
Runner beans e.g. 'Polestar' Supported by a cross cane row
Companion plant e.g. poached-egg plant |

Fabaceae (peas and beans) ✦

Notes:

✦ Family name represents the main group of vegetables in each bed. Some other families may be fitted in for convenience and to make the most of space. Vegetables that are less likely to harbour crop-specific pests and disease are also fitted in throughout.

◆ In cool climates outdoor tomatoes are a gamble; in Scotland cherry varieties tend to perform best. Tomatoes and potatoes are usually grown together in rotation groups but try to separate them if blight is a problem.

◀ Quick-growing plants are sown in between slow growing brassicas and parsnips.

● Radishes are used to mark out two rows of parsnips.

Calendar

These are generic seed-sowing dates for the UK, which will help you start your planning. The season starts later and finishes earlier further north and at higher altitudes so bear in mind your location and check the weather forecast regularly before sowing or transplanting outside.

When to sow, transplant and harvest:
- Sow under glass
- Sow outside/plant outside
- Transplant to final position/transplant outside
- Harvest

Vegetable	Calendar (J F M A M J J A S O N D)	Planting distance between plants	Planting distance between rows	Notes
Aubergine		45-75cm	45-75cm or in a pot	Start earlier sowings in a heated propagator. Will need to be grown under cover in colder climates.
Beetroot		10cm	30cm Sow close together if cropping as salad leaves	Can be slow to germinate, will grow better when soil has warmed up.
Broad bean		20-25cm	25cm	Some varieties are more suitable for overwintering such as 'Aquadulce'. In cold or wet areas sow undercover or indoors in frost-free environment
Broccoli (calabrese) early		60cm	60cm	Harvest before the flower buds open.
Broccoli (calabrese) late		60cm	60cm	Harvest before the flower buds open.
Broccoli (purple sprouting)		60cm	60cm	Grown to overwinter and harvest the following year.
Brussels sprouts		60cm	60cm	Earth up or stake plants to provide support over winter.
Cabbage (spring)		25cm hearted cabbage 15cm for leafy greens	30cm	Plant close together and harvest every other plant as spring greens. Allow remaining cabbages to heart up.
Cabbage (summer)		45cm	45cm	Cut to harvest cabbage then cut a cross on the remaining stump. This will re-sprout new leaves for eating as greens.
Cabbage (winter)		45cm	60cm	Stand well over the winter until required for use.
Carrots		Thin to 5-8cm	30cm	Sow carrots in their final position – they do not like having their roots disturbed. Different varieties are suitable for different sowing times.
Cauliflower (summer/autumn)		45cm	60cm	Require plenty of water at seedling and developing curd growth stages. Cover mature curds with an outer leaf to protect from direct sunshine.
Cauliflower (winter)		60cm	60cm	Protect from bad weather by tying up leaves around curd.
Celeriac		30cm	45cm	Needs warmth to germinate, sow in modules, stores well.
Celery		25cm / 30cm	25cm self-blanching 30cm trench celery	Self-blanching varieties are easier to grow.
Chard		20-25cm	45cm	Overwinter well, may benefit from protection in periods of prolonged frost.
Chicory		25cm / 30cm	30cm Witloof types 30cm red, sugarloaf types	Some chicory varieties can be lifted and placed in a warm dark environment for forcing between autumn and winter.

Vegetable	Spacing (in row)	Spacing (between rows / plants)	Notes
Chillies	40cm	60cm and in pots	Need warm temperatures to germinate. Start earlier sowings in a heated propagator. Will need to be grown under cover in colder climates.
Cucumbers	60cm / 50cm	60cm outdoors / 50cm indoors and in pots	Ridge cucumbers can be grown outside in a sheltered position, sow in late May.
Endive	25cm	30cm	Late sowings will provide leaves until December in mild winters or if protected.
Florence fennel	20-30cm	30cm	Needs plenty of moisture to bulb up and prevent bolting.
French beans	20cm	45cm	Can be started earlier under a cloche but do require protection from frost.
Garlic	15cm	30cm	Plant before Christmas for best yields. Cold weather initiates the bulbing process. Some varieties are suitable for planting in early spring.
Jerusalem artichoke	30cm	30cm	Roots can be stored in the ground over winter until they are needed. They can last until April this way. Grow in a contained area to avoid spreading roots.
Kale	45-60cm	45-60cm	Great overwintering crop and gives architectural structure to plot or garden.
Kohl-rabi	30cm	20cm	Best harvested when golf-ball-sized to avoid woody growth.
Komatsuna	25cm	25–45cm dependent on plant size required. Sow close together for cut-and-come-again plants.	Can be overwintered, but may need protection.
Leeks	15-20cm	30-35cm	Can sow earlier in a propagator for an earlier crop. Keep well in situ until required for eating.
Lettuce	15-30cm	25-40cm dependent on lettuce type and size. Sow close together for cut-and-come-again plants.	Some hardier varieties can be overwintered with protection.
Mange-tout	5cm in single or double rows	60-90cm dependent on height of final plant.	Pick pods regularly to encourage further cropping.
Marrow	90cm	90cm climbing types / 120cm trailing types	Plant out under cloches or frames in late spring.
Mizuna/Mibuna	10-45cm	20-25cm dependent on plant size required. Sow close together for cut-and-come-again plants.	Can be overwintered, may need protection.
Mustard leaves	15-30cm	45cm Sow close together for cut-and-come-again plants.	Can be overwintered, may need protection.
Onion (salad/spring)	2.5cm	30cm	Both overwintering and spring/summer varieties are available.

Month columns: J F M A M J J A S O N D

When to sow, transplant and harvest: ■ Sow under glass   ■ Sow outside/plant outside   ■ Transplant to final position/transplant outside   ■ Harvest

Vegetable	Calendar (J F M A M J J A S O N D)	Planting distance between plants	Planting distance between rows	Notes
Onions from seed		10-15cm dependent on final size required	20-35cm	Growing onions from seed helps to prevent bolting. Amazingly the seeds sown in January will catch up with sets planted out in March/April.
Onions from sets		15cm	20-35cm	If planted too early onions may bolt, remember to plant with enough space for onions to get bigger.
Pak choi		10-45cm	10-45cm depending on variety	Best sown after July to avoid bolting. Can be overwintered, may need protection.
Parsnips		Thin to 15-20cm apart	30cm	Overwinter roots in the ground.
Peas		5cm in single or double rows	60-75cm dependent on height of final plant.	Sow successionally for longer harvest. Round peas are hardier and suitable for very early sowings. Wrinkle pea seeds are sweeter and good for main crop and late harvests.
Peppers		45-50cm	45-50cm and in pots.	Start earlier sowings in a heated propagator. Will need to be grown under cover in colder climates.
Potatoes (first early)		30-35cm	40-50cm	Seed potatoes need chitting.
Potatoes (second early)		35-40cm	60-75cm	Seed potatoes need chitting.
Potatoes (main crop)		35-40cm	75cm	Seed potatoes need chitting.
Pumpkins and winter squashes		90cm / 150cm	90cm bush and trained / 150cm trailing	Require a long growing season so start early undercover and protect outside under a cloche in colder climates.
Radish		1-2cm	15cm	Quick to mature so ideal for successional sowing or intercropping between other slow-growing crops. Also, autumn radishes available for sowing in late summer to extend season.
Rocket		15cm	15cm Sow close together for cut-and-come-again plants.	Quick to mature so ideal for successional sowing. Use thinnings in salads.
Runner beans		15cm at base of wigwam or double row at base of cane supports	60cm	Like a rich soil so prepare a trench early in the season with plenty of organic matter to plant into. Runner beans establish best if sown directly outside in June.
Salsify		Thin to 10cm	15-30cm	Sow from fresh seed as viability deteriorates quickly. Best results are grown on light, sandy soils. Can be left in the soil over winter.
Shallots (sets)		15-20cm	30cm	Some varieties can be planted in December.
Shallots (seed)		Thin to 5cm then to 15cm	30cm	Growing from seed gives better bolt resistance.
Spinach		15cm	30cm	Late sowings in late summer/early autumn provide pickings over winter.
Spinach (perpetual)		20cm	45cm	Can be grown as crop-and-come-again or as a useful winter crop.
Swede		25cm	40cm	Lift when roots are 10-15cm across. Swedes are best stored out of the ground over winter.
Sweetcorn		30-45cm	30-45cm	Will need to be grown in a greenhouse or polytunnel in the northern areas of the UK. Grow in a block formation to aid pollination.

	Sowing/Planting calendar (J F M A M J J A S O N D)	Distance between plants	Notes
Tomatoes	40-45cm vine 30-60cm bush depending on cultivar	90cm vine 90cm bush Also in pots and grow bags.	Require a very sunny, sheltered position. Best grown undercover in colder climates.
Turnip	10-15cm	25-30cm	Extra sweet when harvested young.
Perennial vegetables			
Asparagus (crowns)	15cm / 45cm	30cm / 45cm	Do not harvest in the first year, harvest gradually in subsequent years to allow the plants to establish.
Globe artichoke (seed)	Grow on, then plant as below		Will not crop until July–Sept the following year.
Globe artichoke (Rooted offsets)	90cm	90cm	Plants are easier and quicker to establish from rooted offsets.
Rhubarb	75-90cm	75-90cm	Do not harvest in the first year to allow plant to establish. Different varieties crop from April to August.
Herbs			
Basil	20-30cm	20-30cm	Start earlier sowings in a heated propagator. Will need to be grown undercover in colder climates.
Chives	20-30cm	20-30cm	Will take a year to establish a decent clump from seed. A perennial herb that can be divided each year as clump grows.
Coriander	Thin to 15cm	30cm Sow close together to crop as salad leaves.	Annual herb, successive sowings every 3–4 weeks for a continuous supply over the summer.
Fennel (green/bronze)	Thin to 35-45cm	35-45cm	Perennial herb that looks good in a potager or mixed border.
Lovage	50-60cm	50-60cm	Tall perennial herb useful for flavouring soups.
Oregano	30-40cm	30-40cm	Low-growing perennial herb.
Parsley	20-30cm	20-30cm	Germination is slow, can overwinter with cloche protection, harvest is often better in the second year.
Rosemary	45-60cm	45-60cm	Extremely drought-tolerant perennial herb.
Sage	60-90cm	60-90cm	A perennial, sow seed every 3 or 4 years, or take cuttings as plants become old and woody.
Sorrel	30-45cm	30-45cm	Perennial herb.
Mint	45-90cm	45-90cm	Perennial herb that tolerates shade. Control vigorous roots from spreading by planting mint in a pot and sinking into the soil.
Thyme	45-60cm	45-60cm	Drought-tolerant perennial herb.
Edible flowers – great for pollinating insects			
Calendula	15-25cm	15-25cm	Can also sow in September for flowers the following May–July. Self-seeds readily.
Borage	40-60cm	40-60cm	Flowers can be frozen in ice cubes for summer drinks. Self seeds readily.
Nasturtiums	20-40cm	20-40cm	Flowers and leaves can be eaten in salads. Self-seeds readily.

Preparing your plot

It is very rare to start with a bare, untouched plot when you begin growing vegetables. New plots need to be cleared of vegetation and roots. The simplest method is to dig over the site and remove as many of the roots as possible.

However, perennial weeds can be difficult to eradicate totally. Herbicides can be used as a last resort but it will take several applications to kill weeds. The best organic approach is to cover the plot with a light-excluding mulch – such as cardboard or weed-suppressant fabric, weighed down to prevent it blowing away – and leave it until all the weeds have died. This can take a year or more for long-lived perennial weeds. Rotavators can be useful for clearing plots, but be aware that they can damage soil structure and cut up perennial weed roots into small pieces, effectively propagating them.

Get to know your soil

Your plants source mineral nutrients, air, water, stability and anchorage comes from the soil and if soil is kept healthy it will lead to healthy crops. Soil is a dynamic and complex substance made up of minerals, organic matter, air spaces and living organisms. The type of soil in your garden is determined by the relative proportions of these components.

The mineral component of soil is known as the 'soil texture'. It is made of broken-down bits of rock, which come in the form of sand, silt or clay particles depending on size. Soils that have a proportion of all the different particles are known as loams.

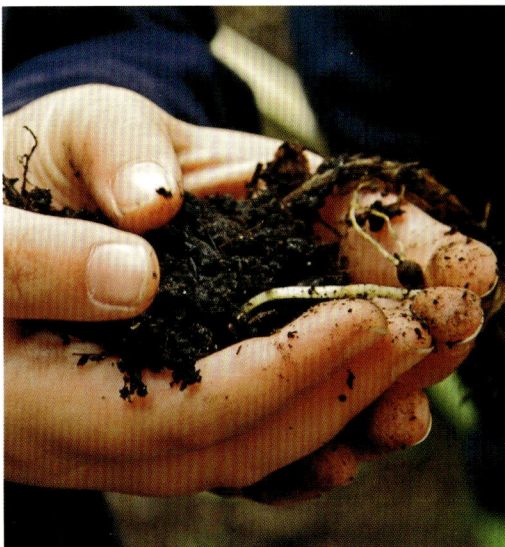

Sandy soil	Particles same size as caster sugar	• Free draining • Poor in nutrients
Silty soil	Particles same size as icing sugar	• Moderately fertile • Moisture-retentive but prone to compaction
Clay soil	Particles ten times smaller than icing sugar	• Particles often stick together • Soils are heavy and often waterlogged but fertile
Peat soil	High proportion of organic matter	• Wet and acidic
Chalk/ limestone soil	Mineral component derived from chalk/limestone	• Moderately fertile • Free draining and alkaline

Soil types

Organic matter in the soil is derived from living things in various states of decay – from fallen leaves to dead insects and animals. Adding organic matter to your soil is the best way of improving it, whatever soil type you have. Sources include manure, garden compost, green manures and leaf mould.

Soil pH

The availability of nutrients to plants is determined by the acidity or alkalinity of the soil. Soils that have developed over a chalk or limestone bedrock tend to be alkaline, while others gradually turn more acidic. The soil acidity also affects soil organisms, pests and disease:

- Worms and beneficial bacteria dislike very acid conditions.
- Clubroot, leatherjackets and wire worms are more common in acid soils.
- Potato scab occurs in alkaline soils.

Most vegetable crops grow best in slightly acidic soil (pH 6.5). You can buy home soil-testing kits or send samples away to advisory services; always test in several places in your garden as the soil will vary.

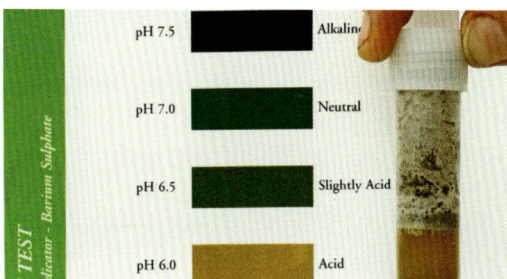

Liming

The most common problem with soil pH in Scotland is high acidity, which can be altered by the addition of lime. This should be used with caution. Apply it as far in advance as possible before planting, and no more than every three to four years. Application is best done in the autumn before planting brassicas, which require a high pH. Do not apply lime and manure at the same time as they will react, producing ammonia which is damaging to plants.

Reducing alkalinity

Increasing the pH is more difficult, although adding organic matter helps. You can also add pine needles or sulphur chips. If your soil is very alkaline, crops that require acidic conditions, such as potatoes and rhubarb, might benefit from being grown in containers or raised beds.

Looking after your soil

Soil profile

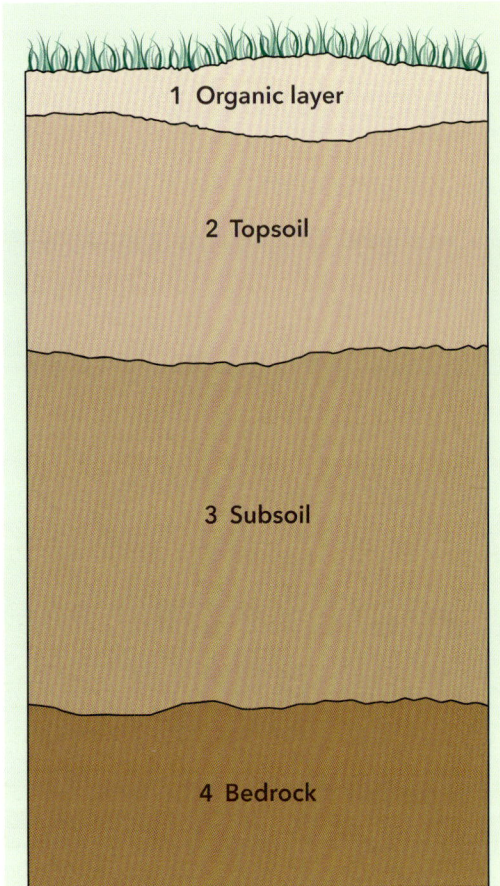

If you dig a deep hole in your soil you may see up to four distinct layers

1 **Organic layer** – decomposing leaves and other organic matter
2 **Topsoil** – containing most of the nutrients and soil organisms
3 **Subsoil** – containing little organic matter and few nutrients
4 **Bedrock**

It is essential that whilst digging, cultivating or levelling your plot you do not mix the topsoil and subsoil, or bring subsoil to the surface. It is deficient in nutrients and will be detrimental to plant growth.

Soil structure

The ideal soil for plant growth has a crumbly structure that allows water and air to filter through. Soil structure is damaged when the particles compress, causing poor drainage and aeration. This is known as compaction and occurs in a number of ways:

- Pans – an impermeable layer of compacted soil forms below the surface.
- Caps – compaction occurs at the soil surface and is due to heavy rain, watering or walking on the soil when it is wet.

Soils can also be eroded by heavy rains, especially when uncovered or free of vegetation.

How to improve soil structure

The first step to improve soil structure is digging and adding organic matter.

Simple digging or forking

Lifting a spade/forkful of soil, turning it over, dropping it back down and breaking it up.

This is useful for removing perennial weeds, and organic matter can be worked in at the same time.

Single digging

- Digging to one spade's depth (known as a 'spit').

- Dig a trench one spit deep and 30cm wide across your plot.

- Pile the soil up out of the way.

- Turn the soil from the next trench into the first whilst creating a new one.

- Continue doing this until the whole plot has been 'dug'.

- You can fork in organic matter during this process.

Double digging

Cultivation to two spades' depth. This is only necessary where the soil is heavily compacted. In this method, the first and second spit are turned independently to ensure subsoil is not brought to the surface.

'No dig'

Digging can cause damage to the natural soil structure and increase weed germination. In this method, organic mulches are applied directly to the soil surface, preferably in autumn. They are worked into the soil naturally by earthworms and other organisms. If the soil structure is damaged or infected with perennial weeds, carry out an initial dig before mulching.

Creating a tilth

This is the last stage of preparation of the ground before seed is sown. Tilth is composed of small (breadcrumb-sized), even soil particles that absorb water easily and allow seeds to germinate. Create this by going over the soil with a fork, hoe or rake to break up the clods and level the surface. Then gently rake the soil over with a push-pull action, removing any stones or debris. For finer seed, such as carrots and brassicas, a finer consistency is required whereas larger beans and peas can tolerate a coarser consistency.

Green manures/ mulches

This is the term given to plants grown especially to improve or protect soil structure. They can be sown throughout the growing season and are ideal on land that will be free of crops for several months. Let the plants grow for around through the winter, or until they start to flower, then dig them into the soil. Leave them to decompose in the soil for four weeks before growing vegetables. Sow winter hardy varieties in August and September to overwinter in empty vegetable plots. Winter grazing rye (*Secale cereale*) or winter tares/vetch (*Vicia sativa*) are good, as is phacelia (*Phacelia tanacetifolia*); this isn't fully hardy but if frosts kill it you can leave the plants *in situ,* protecting the soil.

Vegetable garden layout

The best method of cultivating vegetables is in permanent, narrow – approximately 1.2m – beds, divided by a network of permanent paths, although vegetables can be laid out in rows across an open plot. A timber edge is ideal for defining the edge of beds and to contain the soil and organic matter that builds up.

- All work on the plot can be done from the pathways, protecting the soil structure.

- Narrow beds lend themselves to intense planting regimes, with little room for weeds to germinate.

- Having beds defined makes crop rotations easier.

Tools

There are many gardening tools available; here is some information on the basics. The tools we think are necessary for getting started are in bold.

Choosing tools

- Make sure tools are the right height and weight for you by trying them out in the shop to check that they feel comfortable.
- Buy the best you can afford; cheap tools are often a false economy.

Tool maintenance

Take care of your tools:

- Wipe down after use with an oily cloth to prevent rusting.
- Keep hoes and spades sharp using a carborundum stone or file.
- Keep tools undercover to prevent damage from the weather.

Tool	Uses
Spade	Digging and moving soil
Fork	Preparing soil, forking soil, turning compost, lifting crops
Garden rake	Preparing seed beds, removing stones/debris
Hoes **Dutch** (also known as push hoe) Draw **Oscillating**	Weeding, creating sowing drills, drawing up earth The Dutch hoe is pushed just under the soil surface to cut through weeds as the gardener walks backwards The draw hoe is pulled towards the gardener in a chopping action The oscillating hoe has a razor sharp blade that travels below the soil surface and slices through the weeds; long handle allows you to reach in amongst vegetable beds without trampling on them
Trowel	Planting out, weeding
Hand fork	Weeding, loosening soil
Watering can with various roses (nozzle heads)/hand sprayer	Watering, applying liquid fertilisers and biological controls (nematodes)
Wheelbarrow/**trug**	Moving material, weeds, composts and mulches
Secateurs	Cutting down finished crops (cabbage, tomatoes, etc.) for composting
Scissors/garden knife	Harvesting salad crops, cutting string
Garden line (string and canes)	Marking seed rows/planting
Gardening gloves	Protecting hands
Kneeling pad or knee pads	Protecting knees when weeding and planting

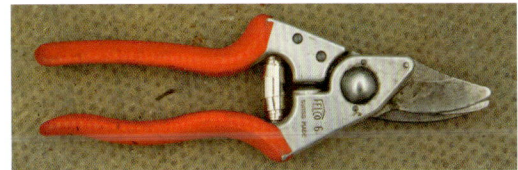

Wildlife in the vegetable garden

There are many beneficial organisms that visit the vegetable garden and if you encourage them they will help to keep your garden healthy.

Organisms that eat aphids:

- Hoverfly larvae
- Parasitic wasps
- Ladybirds

Organisms that break down organic matter in the soil, releasing plant nutrients:

- Earthworms – also help to create good soil structure
- Some slugs – a vital part of the composting process
- Woodlice – sometimes also eat living plants and seedlings
- Bacteria and fungi in the soil

Organisms that eat slugs and snails:

- Birds
- Frogs, toads and newts
- Hedgehogs

Pollinators – help to ensure good harvests of fruit crops such as peas, beans and courgettes:

- Bees and wasps
- Hoverflies

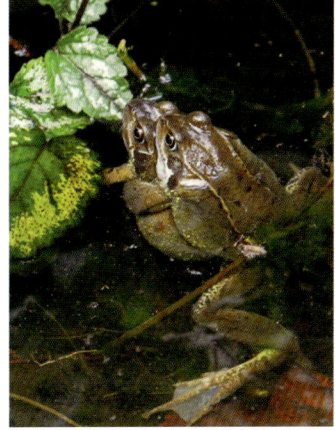

Organisms that eat insects:

- Bats
- Birds
- Spiders
- Centipedes

Organisms that eat caterpillars:

- Birds – a pair of blue tits require 10,000 caterpillars and other insects to rear one brood of chicks
- Parasitic wasps

Organisms that eat soil pests:

- Birds
- Frogs
- Ground beetles

How to attract beneficial wildlife

- Grow a wide range of flowers to attract pollinators and predatory insects such as ladybirds and hoverflies – they also look great! Include nasturtiums, poached-egg plant, marigolds, sweet peas or sunflowers.
- A patch of long grass, shrubs, hedges and trees near your vegetable patch will provide a valuable habitat and nesting sites for a range of organisms.
- Feed the birds and install nest boxes.
- Construct homes for lacewings and solitary bees.
- Ponds provide breeding sites for frogs, toads and newts.
- Build a habitat pile from dead wood.
- Compost heaps are not only a great way of providing nutrients for your garden, they also shelter beneficial organisms.
- Leave a few carrots and cabbages to flower – aphid-eating hoverflies love them.
- Herbs like borage, chives, fennel, lavender, mint and sage attract beneficial insects.
- Protect hedgehogs and blackbirds by avoiding using slug pellets.

Gardens play an increasingly important role in safeguarding biodiversity, so think carefully before you reach for pesticides.

Buying and saving seeds

Vegetables can be grown from seed or bought as immature plants from garden centres and mail-order catalogues. Buying young plants is often considered an easier option for beginners but don't be put off growing from seed.

Advantages of growing from seed

- A wider variety of crops are available.
- Seeds are cheaper to buy than plants.
- You are in control of the quality, origin and growing method (for example, organic).
- They can be grown successfully, ensuring a continuous crop (see p. 26).
- They are less likely to harbour pests and diseases.
- Some plants (such as carrots and parsnips) don't like being transplanted.

Disadvantages of growing from seed

- More effort and time is required.
- Suitable conditions need to be provided for germination.
- Newly germinated seedlings are easy to over- or under-water.
- It is easy to end up with too many plants.

Pollination

Pollination occurs when pollen from the male part of the flower, the anther, attaches to the female part of the flower, the stigma. The pollen grains fertilise the eggs and go on to form seed. Some plants can pollinate themselves and produce viable seed, like peas. Others need to cross-pollinate, with pollen fertilising the eggs on a different plant, transferred by insects or the wind. Some plants both self- and cross-pollinate. Cross-pollinating plants produce seed that has a variety of characteristics and resulting plants are unlikely to be the same as the parent. To keep cross pollinators 'pure', plants of the same variety will need to be isolated to prevent pollination from other varieties.

If you are saving seed from a cross-pollinating plant you will need to try and control where the pollen comes from. If a flower is cross-pollinated with a different variety of plant the resulting seed will not be uniform.

Heritage varieties

Heritage varieties are also known as heirloom or traditional varieties. They tend to be older kinds of fruits and vegetables, not widely used in commercial growing. The commercialisation of vegetable growing, seed legislation and the development of F1 hybrids have all impacted on the number of heritage varieties available. These are important as they are more genetically diverse than F1 hybrids. The risk of only growing genetically similar plants is that they are susceptible to the same threats; disease or unfavourable weather conditions can destroy an entire crop. Growing heritage varieties may save valuable genetic traits for the future and importantly, those which are grown locally will have been selected over generations for performing well in that location.

F1 hybrids

An F1 hybrid is the result of crossing two purebred varieties. These are selected and grown for their vigour and uniformity, and are favoured by mechanised growers and large commercial seed companies for this reason. They can be bred for a specific trait, such as frost hardiness, which can be useful to a home grower. F1 hybrids are bred to crop all at the same time for commercial harvest, which can lead to unwanted gluts for the home grower. Seed saved from an F1 hybrid will have a variety of characteristics and not be the same as the parent plants.

Saving seed examples

Tomatoes

- Allow fruits to ripen on the plant.
- Once the fruit is ripe, harvest and remove the seeds.
- Remove the growth inhibitor coating on the seeds by soaking them in water for about three days. Allow to ferment and stir regularly.
- Rinse well and drain.
- Spread out to dry on a hard surface.

French beans

- Allow the pods to mature and then dry naturally on the plant.
- Harvest and finish the drying off inside.
- Remove the beans from the pod.

Kale

Kale is an example of a crop that it is much harder to save seed from. It is biennial – it flowers in its second year – so you have to keep the plant in the ground for longer in order for it to produce seed. Kale also cross-pollinates very easily, so to guarantee seed purity plants must be grown at least a mile away from other brassicas in flower. You can isolate the plants of the same variety in a mesh cage to keep out insects that might have visited other varieties. However, you will need to introduce some insects into the cage to pollinate your desired crop.

- You should get lots of seed from even a few plants (although the genetic diversity will be greatest where large numbers are grown).
- After the plant has flowered leave the stalks in place for the seed to ripen and dry.
- Harvest the seed directly from the plant or cut the stalks when they start to turn brown, and continue to dry them inside.

Storage and viability

Store all seeds in paper envelopes in an airtight container once completely dry, and keep in a cool dark place. You can add a little dry rice to the container to soak up any excess moisture. All seed will lose its viability over time; carrots and parsnips lose theirs particularly quickly and can only be stored for a year. Brassica seeds last longer and if stored correctly can last for several years.

Sowing and transplanting

Once you have planned your crops for the season there are a few things to consider before you begin to sow. Different methods suit different crops so it is worth knowing various techniques before you start.

Seeds need:

- **Warmth**
  Few vegetables will germinate below 5°C, but many require 15–20°C or more (sweetcorn, courgettes and tomatoes).

- **Light/darkness**
  Seeds should be covered to approximately twice their depth, so fine seeds are just covered (carrots, parsnips, lettuce) and large seeds (beans, peas, sweetcorn) sown deeper.

- **Air and moisture**
  Oxygen, carbon dioxide and water help break dormancy. The correct balance can be supplied by using a growing medium that is both well-drained and moisture-retentive.

Outdoor sowing

Outdoor sowing techniques

- **Drill/row sowing**
  Seeds are sown in narrow rows or flat-bottomed trenches. Mark out a straight line using string and canes or use the edge of a wooden board as a guide. Then create the drill by drawing a cane, hoe or trowel through the soil. The depth will depend on which seeds you are sowing. Wide drills can be used to position larger seeds at correct distances, forming several rows of the same vegetable (peas, beans), or to grow a wider patch of salad leaves.

- **Station sowing/space sowing**
  Place seeds individually or in small groups, with pre-determined spacing along a row. This is good for easy-to-handle seeds (parsnips, beetroots, turnips).

- **Broadcast sowing**
  Scatter the seeds over the soil surface to cover a block area, then gently rake to ensure they are buried. This is good for crops that do not require thinning (cut-and-come-again salad crops and green manures).

How to sow outdoors

- Ensure the soil temperature is at least 7°C.
- Use a board to spread your weight over the soil.
- Place the seeds in the palm of your hand. Take small pinches to help control the number and placement of the seeds along the row.
- Always try to sow thinly.
- Once completed, rake the soil or scatter compost thinly over the top. Using compost to cover the seed helps to mark out the row and distinguish the germinating crop from weeds.
- Use a garden rake on end to gently press the soil in contact with the seed.
- Always water thoroughly using a fine-spray watering can.
- Label your row.

Thinning

Once your seedlings grow you will need to remove some to provide more space, light and ventilation for those remaining.

- Thin out when plants are young to minimise damage to remaining seedlings.
- Pinch out seedlings at the base of the stem.
- Water after thinning to settle soil back round the remaining seedlings.
- Thin in stages to achieve the correct plant spacing.

Remember

- Sowing into wet and cold soil will result in poor germination; wait until conditions are right.
- Avoid sowing on a windy day when seeds can blow around.
- In wet weather, cover the ground prior to sowing to dry the soil.
- In dry weather, water the drill prior to sowing.
- Mix fine seeds with horticultural sand to ensure a more sparse distribution when sowing.
- Sow seeds thinly to avoid waste, overcrowding and time wasted thinning.
- Weed regularly.

Indoor sowing

Things to consider

Growing medium/compost

This needs to be:

- Sterile (to prevent disease)
- Open in structure, to allow air and water to percolate easily
- Moisture-retentive (to allow seeds to absorb water)
- Low in nutrients (to avoid scorching roots or encouraging soft sappy growth)

Containers

- Take into account the depth of the eventual root system and speed of growth
- Plants that do not like root disturbance can be sown in modules, for example beans, celeriac, swede and fennel

Growing environment

- Ensure a heat source is available (windowsill, propagator, greenhouse) for seeds such as aubergines and chillies

Potential problems indoors

- Fungal diseases can kill seedlings. Always use clean pots and fresh sterile compost, and avoid excessive watering.
- Seedlings become elongated (leggy) if light conditions are poor.
- Don't sow root crops like parsnips/carrots indoors as their tap roots dislike being disturbed.

Tips

- Place a piece of silver foil behind your trays to reflect light and turn them daily to prevent lopsided growth.
- Save money by making sowing pots from empty toilet rolls, paper and plastic containers; always add drainage holes.
- Sow tender crops five to six weeks before your last expected frost.

How to sow indoors

1 Overfill the pot/tray with fresh seed compost.

2 Level off any excess compost and tap the container so that the compost sinks slightly.

3 Create a flat even surface by gently pressing the compost lightly with a flat board.

4 Sow your seeds.*

5 Cover the seeds lightly with compost using a sieve.

6 Label your container with the variety and date.

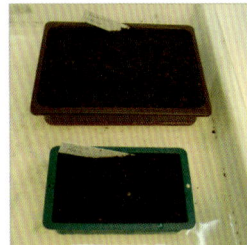

7 Place trays/pots containing fine seeds in a water trough to absorb liquid from the base until the compost surface turns a shade darker.

8 Water larger seeds from overhead using a fine spray. After sowing cover trays with a clear plastic bag to prevent moisture loss; avoid direct sunlight.

*Fine seeds should be sown evenly (broadcast) over the surface. Larger seeds can be positioned individually (space sown) by pushing the seed to the correct depth.

Transplanting seedlings

Pricking out

Once seedlings are large enough to handle (when they have produced two true leaves) pot them into larger containers to allow space for root development. Be careful – damaging the stem can kill the seedling so always lift them by their leaves.

- Prepare your containers and fill with compost.
- Create a hole with a dibber.
- Carefully lift individual or small groups of seedlings by holding their leaves and supporting the roots with the dibber.
- Use the dibber to direct the roots into the hole.
- Gently fill with compost to cover the roots.
- Water in using a fine spray.
- Place seedlings back into the same growing environment to prevent shock.

Potting on

Certain vegetables may require further potting into a larger container before planting out in their final growing position. Courgettes, tomatoes, sweetcorn and pumpkins are often grown on in this way. Observe each plant and examine the root growth. If roots are becoming congested (growing out the base of their pot) it is time to move the plant into a larger container.

Hardening off

This term describes preparing a plant for its final growing conditions outside.

- Place plants sown indoors out into a cold frame or a sheltered spot during the day for a couple of hours.
- Extend the period of exposure each day.
- Eventually leave the plants out overnight; they can be covered with horticultural fleece if night temperatures suddenly dip.
- After two weeks the plants are ready for planting in their final position.
- Keep an eye on the weather forecast and pick mild conditions to start this process.

Planting out

A plant is ready for planting out when the root system holds the growing medium together but the roots are not pot-bound. For tender crops such as courgettes, runner beans and tomatoes, wait until the danger of frost has passed.

- Prepare the soil, removing weed competition.
- Mark out where each plant is to be placed (based on final plant size).
- Dig a hole slightly larger than the plant's pot.
- Add organic matter where crops require a moisture-retentive soil (courgettes, runner beans).
- Gently remove the plant, place in the hole and gently fill to cover the roots.
- Firm the soil with your hands and water well.
- Mulch with compost to suppress weeds and lock in moisture.
- Protect initially with cloches or fleece if required.

Tips

- Growth can be stunted if plants are not acclimatised properly to their final growing positions.
- Water plants thoroughly both before planting out and again once in position. Avoid planting on windy days as this can dry out the root system and weaken the plant.
- On heavy soils mound your plant slightly above ground level to prevent waterlogging.
- On dry soils set the plant deeper so water can collect near the roots.

Looking after your crops

Plants need to be monitored on a regular basis. Look out for:

- Water supply
- Overcrowding
- Weeds
- Feeding

Young plants are especially vulnerable and indoor seedlings need to be checked every day.

Watering

Indicators of under- and over-watering

Too much water

- Water pools on soil surface.
- There are signs of rot/fungal and green algae growth on soil surface.
- Roots die back, causing flowers to drop, leaves to turn yellow and growth to stop.
- Pot is heavy.

Too little water

- The plant wilts and has limp leaves and stems.
- Soil is a pale colour.
- Growing medium has pulled away from the pot.
- Pot is very light.

Techniques to get it right

- Check the moisture beneath the soil surface with your finger to assess watering requirements.
- Adjust the watering regime depending on the expected temperature, sunshine and wind levels.
- Water early in the morning or late in the evening to minimise loss due to evaporation.
- Soaking plants thoroughly once a week is better than frequent, light watering. This is likely to evaporate without reaching the plant and can lead to the formation of shallow roots, making plants susceptible to drought.
- Use an appropriate irrigation method for the plant (fine spray on delicate plants, hose spray on large established plants).
- In areas of low rainfall, grow crops that are less susceptible to drought, such as chard, onions, garlic and perennials such as rhubarb, asparagus, rosemary, thyme and artichokes.
- Use raised beds where waterlogging is prevalent.
- Raise pots off the ground on feet to aid drainage and avoid them standing in water.
- Add water-retentive granules to the soil or compost.
- Remove weeds that compete for moisture.

Water-saving tips

- Target water to the roots by sinking a pot or upturned bottomless plastic bottle beside the plant. Water directly into the bottle.
- Create a trench, or mound soil around plants to direct water to the roots.
- Mulch around the plant with materials such as bark chips, leaf mould, compost or straw, applying mulch after watering to lock in moisture.
- Collect rainwater in butts from sheds, greenhouses and buildings.
- Water used for cleaning vegetables and washing up can be used intermittently (to prevent chemical build-up) on established plants.
- Improve the soil's ability to hold moisture and drain freely by adding organic matter during soil preparation.

Feeding

Plants require nutrients from the soil to maintain healthy growth. Nitrogen (N), phosphorus (P) and potassium (K), known as N:P:K, are needed in large amounts and are found in 'general' fertilisers. Plants also need magnesium (Mg), calcium (Ca) and sulphur (S), as well as various trace elements (iron, manganese, molybdenum, zinc, copper and boron) in smaller amounts. These are generally readily available in the soil; however, extreme acid or alkaline conditions can lock up certain nutrients, so check the soil pH.

Feeding methods

- Base dressing – a general fertiliser with an even N:P:K ratio can be applied during soil preparation to give plants a good start.

- Top dressing – provides an extra boost once crops are growing. Good for plants with higher nitrogen requirements such as brassicas, or fruit crops with increased potassium needs, such as tomatoes.

- Foliar feed (applied to leaves) – used to counteract any general nutrient deficiencies and supply trace elements with immediate effect.

Feeding tips

Certain crops benefit from extra feeds when:

- Fruits are developing – weekly potassium feeds will benefit chillies and tomatoes.

- Growing 'hungry crops' such as brassicas, potatoes, courgettes and pumpkins.

- Plants look unwell – pep them up with a seaweed drench rich in trace nutrients.

- Pot plants exhaust their available nutrients. Repot in fresh compost and top dress with a slow-release fertiliser.

What to apply

Organic

These are derived from a natural source of carbon (animal or plant material). Generally the nutrients are released more slowly than inorganic fertilisers.

Bulky forms
- Farmyard manure
- Garden compost
- Green manures (see p. 40)

Concentrated forms
- Manure pellets – these are nitrogen rich
- Fish, blood and bone – high P, medium N but low K value
- Ash – wood ashes are high in potassium
- Seaweed – a good source of micronutrients
- Compost teas can be made by soaking leaves of nutrient-rich plants (comfrey/nettle) or manure
- Liquid from wormeries (see p. 57)

Inorganic

These are chemicals containing no carbon. They are fast-acting and easy to handle, store and spread, but excessive use can lead to nutrients leaching and harming soil organisms.

Concentrated forms

- Ammonium salts – nitrogen
- Potassium salts – potassium
- Phosphate salts – phosphorus

These can be applied as:

- Individual fertilisers to provide a specific nutrient.
- Compound fertilisers to provide varying quantities of essential nutrients.
- Controlled-release fertilisers (CRF) to disperse nutrients over a set period of time.

◄ Wormeries

- Wormeries can be bought commercially or constructed at home. They consist of containers that stack together in layers and house worms that can compost a variety of waste materials.

- The worms are placed in the lower layers and move up the unit towards the waste material as it is added at the top. As the worms move up they leave worm casts behind. The casts can be harvested and make excellent compost.

- In addition to casts the wormery will produce a liquid, collected from the base of the unit, that can be used as a plant fertiliser. Commercially made wormeries have a tap at the base for this purpose. It is quite strong so should be diluted one part liquid to ten parts water.

- Wormeries are an excellent option for composting kitchen waste in a small garden. Worms can compost materials from kitchen vegetable peelings to the contents of a vacuum cleaner bag. They don't like very acidic conditions, however, so avoid adding citrus. It is best to add small quantities frequently; wormeries are not suitable for large volumes of garden waste.

Crop protection

Part of the ongoing maintenance of your plot is likely to include protecting your crops. Reasons for protecting plants include:

- Providing shelter from the elements (wind, heavy rain, hail, snow and frost).

- Trapping and providing warmth to extend the growing season, bring forward and lengthen harvests, and increase the range of plants grown (tender crops such as tomatoes, cucumbers and aubergines).

- Forming a barrier to pests (insects, birds, mammals) and diseases (tomato blight).

Points to note

- Protected plants require extra time and care to provide the correct growing conditions (watering, ventilation and good light quality).

- A protected environment can increase the likelihood of certain pests and diseases due to warmth, humidity and poor air movement.

Protection techniques

Pest protection

Covering plants with:
- Fine thread or twiggy branches can be a good deterrent against birds.
- Extremely fine mesh and fleece will protect against insects, whilst more open netting stops damage by birds and mammals.
- Chicken wire will protect against rabbits and deer.
- Open baskets or structures made from willow or birch will stop animals disturbing the crops and provide some frost protection.

A cloche, glasshouse or polytunnel will also provide varying degrees of pest protection, although if pests do establish they can be difficult to control.

Vegetables in the carrot family are often grown under fleece or fine mesh for their entire lifecycle to prevent carrot root fly laying eggs on the soil next to the crop.

Shelter and warmth

Floating mulches

- **Polythene films** – cover the soil to protect against erosion and weed growth and to warm the soil prior to sowing or planting. They can be made of clear, black, white or perforated plastic.

- **Horticultural fleece** – a non-woven, permeable fabric made from polypropylene that insulates crops against frost and protects against certain pests (carrot root fly, cabbage fly, moths and flea beetle). It is available in various weights to provide different levels of frost protection. Fleece can be used as a ground cover to warm the soil for emerging seedlings or shaped into a low tent to provide protection throughout the crop's life.

Cloches

Cloche means 'bell' in French and originally referred to glass shelter placed over crops. It now means any structure that covers a plant to give some form of protection. Cloches come in various forms referred to according to their shape (tent, barn, tunnel, lantern and bell). They can be purchased or made at home using some of the following materials:

- **Cover materials** – glass (caution: can easily be damaged), plastic films, rigid plastics, empty plastic bottles, horticultural fleece, netting, mesh or plant material (willow)

- **Support materials** – wood, bricks, metal hoops (coat hangers, wire, clips), plastic hoops (such as flexible water pipes), canes or plant stems (willow, birch)

A good cloche should:

- Allow light into the growing seedlings/plants.
- Trap heat, but provide adequate ventilation when required.
- Be large enough that plants do not touch the sides, to avoid condensation dripping on leaves or freezing in cold weather.
- Be robust in high winds, but easy to move, handle and fold away for storage, irrigation, weeding and cropping access.
- Fit the cropping area, or adapt to the final size and height of plants.

Securing cloches

- Prevent covers from blowing away by tucking the covering material into the soil and weighing it down with wooden boards, bags of sand or bricks. String attached to weights can also be used to hold cloches in position.
- Cloche edges can be pinned down with metal, plastic pegs or even twigs.
- Prevent wind from tunnelling through cloches by sealing the ends.

Watering

- Many materials (perforated plastics, horticultural fleece) are permeable and allow water to pass through. Some covers are made from watertight materials but can still provide moisture by absorption from irrigation supplied from outside the edge of the cloche. However, it may be necessary to remove cloches and water when the soil becomes dry.

Weed growth

- A warm environment will encourage your vegetables to grow quickly. It will have the same effect on weeds too. Consider plant spacing to allow a hoe to pass between rows, or stepping stones in strategic places to allow access for hand weeding.

At RBGE the first-year HND/BSc Horticulture with Plantsmanship students are encouraged to use cloches to bring forward plant growth for their early assessment date on the student plots. Every year students create more ingenious and creative structures to protect their plants.

Cold frames

Cold frames are:

- In between cloches and glasshouses in terms of size and climate control.
- Used mainly to 'bring on' and 'harden off' young seedlings and plants.
- Often made from wood or brick with a moveable glass or transparent plastic top to maximise light and ventilation.
- Sometimes permanent, sometimes moveable fixtures.
- Often adapted to grow plants right through to harvest, or combined with a 'hotbed' to provide extra warmth through the plant's lifecycle.

Windowsills

Seedlings can be started off successfully inside on a well-lit windowsill. East- or north-facing windows are best to regulate fluctuations in temperature and prevent scorching of young seedlings. It is a great way to start off tender crops (tomatoes, cucumbers, chillies and aubergines) or slow-growing crops (onions from seed, leeks, celery and celeriac) that require a long growing season. A few plants can be successfully grown to harvest inside with relatively low light levels (cucumbers, chillies, herbs and micro salads).

Conservatories

Conservatories tend to have better light levels than windowsills and also higher temperatures due to their common south- or west-facing aspect. They are a good alternative to growing plants in a glasshouse, especially for tender crops.

- Remember to ensure adequate ventilation is available on hot days.
- Pests can be difficult to control if a problem does arise.

Polytunnels and glasshouses

These larger sheltered environments are the ultimate in crop protection. Good light quality and easily controllable conditions allow you to grow more tender crops all year round. Further cloches or covers can be installed inside to provide additional protection in cold snaps, and plants can be cultivated off the ground in grow bags or pots. Both structures can be heated if required and you can further extend the season with early and late sowings.

Disadvantages include the following:

- The initial installation cost is high.
- Heating is expensive if the structure is maintained as a frost-free area.
- Daily maintenance is required to regulate extremes of temperature, control ventilation and for general watering and feeding of plants.
- Seasonal maintenance is required to keep glass clean or shaded and structurally sound.
- Heavy snowfalls need to be cleared quickly to prevent structural damage.

At RBGE we have a fantastic polytunnel where we grow and propagate a wide range of crops, including:

- Winter salads
- Tender summer vegetables such as tomatoes, chillies and climbing French beans

We are also able to start growing crops earlier and keep harvesting them later in the season.

- A good layout is essential for a productive and accessible tunnel.
- A wide central path provides excellent access for students, volunteers, school groups, members of the public and staff who work in the tunnel.
- Two-thirds of the polytunnel is laid out with beds where crops are grown directly in the soil.
- One-third is taken up by benches where we propagate seedlings to be planted out in the tunnel and in our outdoor beds.

Keeping a close eye on the weather forecast is vital for planning ventilation and watering in a polytunnel. Vigilance, fast action and good hygiene are key to keeping pests and disease under control. We have three resident frogs that help to keep the slugs at bay.

Support and training

There are several reasons why you might introduce support and training methods in your vegetable garden. They can:

- Maintain plants with climbing or upright habits.
- Maximise available sunlight, air and warmth.
- Support plants with heavy crops.
- Prevent plants collapsing after heavy rain or strong winds.
- Maximise available space in a small area.
- Make harvesting easier (create a better height for picking and to avoid soil contamination).
- Produce a decorative and functional display.
- Create shade or a screen.

Materials for support

The support needs to be strong and stable to take the weight of the fully grown plant. The material should be slightly flexible and open to allow air movement through the structure.

Supports can be made from:

- **Man-made materials**
  Plastic netting, metal hoops and poles, linked wire supports, wire trellis, chicken wire, coated wire

- **Natural materials**
  Willow, birch, hazel, dogwood and other twiggy branches (for pea sticks); wooden arches, existing fences, pergolas, obelisks, natural trellis, wigwams, bamboo cane structures tied together with string, open jute/hessian netting placed vertically or at an angle

It is a good idea to dry twigs such as willow, hazel and dogwood for a season before using them as supports. If the twigs are used immediately after they have been cut they can continue to grow and compete with your crops.

▼ The HND/BSc first-year students make use of the natural materials available within the Garden to produce sympathetic and sustainable plant supports. Birch and willow are favoured because of their ability to be woven into almost any shape or size. They also make attractive features in themselves.

Support methods

- Pea sticks (any twiggy branches that provide support) should be positioned before the seeds are sown. ▶

- Plants that do not naturally cling may require tying in with string, clips or soft ties (strips of old tights/cloth). Avoid tying too tightly as this can damage or break stems at the point of contact. A figure-of-eight loop allows the plant to expand and minimises the risk of snapping in the wind.

- Plant crops such as broad beans and peas in blocks or rows to allow the plants to support themselves.

- Strong upright plants (such as sunflowers) can be used to support other climbing plants, for example climbing beans or peas.

- Nets can be stretched horizontally or at an angle through canes to support climbing or trailing plants like squash or courgettes.

- Tomatoes are often supported by wrapping string around the plant root ball and then connecting the other end to an overhead glasshouse fitting. The plant stem can be gently wound around the string as it grows.

- Canes can be used to support individual plants as required, for example Brussels sprouts over winter, or to form structures that support multiple plants, such as peas or climbing beans.

Training techniques

Pruning methods

These are used to control the shape, size and growth habit of the plant.

Stopping

Pinching off the top growth once a plant has reached the desired height to control overall size (tomatoes).

Pinching out

Removing young growth or fruits, often just using your fingers and thumb in order to:

- Concentrate production on remaining fruits and flowers to develop fewer, but better quality, crops (melon, cucumber, peppers).
- Remove soft growth that is more susceptible to pest attack (aphids on broad beans) or late frost damage.
- Encourage a bushier habit (chillies).

Thinning

Removing excess fruit that the plant would not be able to sustain if left. This allows plants to develop fewer, but healthier and better sized, individual fruits (cucumber, melons, peppers).

Points to remember

- Support and stake plants whilst they are young to achieve the best results. This minimises root disturbance and gives plants support as they grow. It also avoids time wasting, potential plant damage and inconvenience if crops are supported adequately at the start.
- Try to anticipate the growth rate and habit of each plant and stake/support appropriately.
- Ensure that structures are secured firmly, especially tall supports, and that they will hold the final harvest. A lot of structures can double up as supports for protection too.

Harvesting and storage

Knowing when to harvest crops and how to store them is one of the skills involved in growing vegetables. This knowledge will allow you to keep your kitchen stocked with home-grown produce through the colder months and the 'hungry gap'.

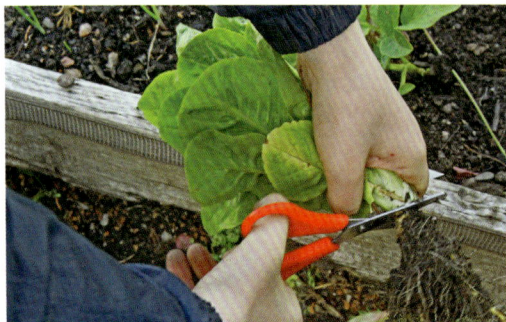

Tips for successful harvesting

- Harvest when crops are fully ripe and in peak condition.
- Gather plants first thing to avoid moisture loss on warm or windy days, or close to your cooking time for freshness.
- Use a sharp knife, scissors or secateurs to minimise damage to remaining plants.
- Seal salad crops in a plastic bag or box to prevent moisture loss. Other crops are best placed in paper or cloth bags to allow them to breathe.
- Allow soil to dry on root crops then rub or rinse it off. This helps protect the fine skins on potatoes, carrots and beetroots.
- Compost plant tops and roots.
- Don't wash vegetables intended for storage. Soil contains good bacteria that will help preserve them for longer.

Storing

Each vegetable will require slightly different storage conditions but generally they need a dry, cool (frost-free) and well-ventilated space, of even temperature and free from pests.

Leave plants in position

Certain crops can be left in their growing position until required for harvest, such as cabbage, kale, sprouts, parsnips, leeks and Jerusalem artichokes. This is a good method unless severe frosts are forecast.

Outside storage

Heeling in – Vegetables are lifted with their roots still attached and placed into a V-shaped trench that is then filled with loose soil. This will keep them fresh but protected from heavy frost until required.

Clamp – An old method used to store root vegetables such as carrots, beetroot, turnips and potatoes. Place the roots on a bed of straw and stack them in layers to form a pile. Cover the vegetables with more straw and a layer of soil. This protects the roots from rain and frost whilst allowing ventilation. Check regularly for slugs, mice and disease.

Inside storage

Root crops can be stored in a cool and dry place (shed, unheated room or porch). Place roots in hessian sacks or cardboard boxes to exclude light or in shallow boxes containing slightly moist sand, coir, sieved soil or fine sawdust. Only store crops in perfect condition and check them regularly, removing any with signs of mould or rot. Some crops, such as pumpkins, can store well like this for up to six months.

Drying

Many crops can be preserved through slow drying in the sun, in an oven or undercover in an airy place. Crops suitable for this treatment are garlic, herbs, chillies and tomatoes. Herbs and chillies can be strung up and slow-dried in a warm airy place before storing in a tin or jar. Plait onions and garlic onto string to make an attractive display. Peas and beans can be left to dry on the plant before shelling seeds to store in an airtight jar. The peas can then be rehydrated and used for cooking at a later date.

Freezing

Blanch vegetables in boiling water for one minute, cool quickly and dry before spreading thinly on a tray to freeze. Once part-frozen (20 minutes) produce can be placed into a freezer bag and labelled. Beans, peas, broccoli, kale, courgettes and tomatoes can be frozen successfully, as is true for most vegetables. The textures can alter though, and making soups and sauces can help to hide this. Herbs can be frozen: chop finely, place in ice-cube trays, and cover with water then freeze. Frozen foods store well for around six months.

Preserving

A good way to use up excess produce is to preserve as pickles, chutneys and conserves by adding vinegar, salt, sugar and spices. Once preserved, most vegetables last for 12 months.

Pests, diseases and disorders

Occasionally you may experience problems with your crop in the form of pests, diseases or disorders that can affect your yield. Most are easily manageable with a little know-how. Learn to tolerate some damage. By attempting to destroy all pests you may harm beneficial animals and upset the natural balance in your garden. Chemicals, if used, should always be a last resort.

Identifying pests and diseases

Regular inspection allows you to monitor and notice any changes to your plants. If a plant looks unwell note any symptoms and look for any pests. Place any affected parts in a plastic bag or take photographs for later identification indoors.

Control methods

Pests and diseases are generally managed by one or a combination of the following methods.

Cultural
- Good plant management, for example correct spacing, feeding and watering
- Good gardening hygiene
- Awareness of pest or disease lifecycle (sowing vegetables at specific times within a pest/disease lifecycle can minimise potential damage)

Physical
- Hand removal of pest or infected plant part
- Traps, deterrents and barriers to prevent contact

Biological
Biological methods control pests in the following ways:
- Introducing a natural predator or parasite to control the pest
- Companion planting to attract beneficial insects or confuse pests away from particular crops

Chemical
Chemicals control pests in the following ways:
- The pest is killed on immediate contact with a chemical
- Systemic pesticides – the chemical is absorbed into the plant then the pest feeds on it

Both non-organic and organic chemicals can negatively affect beneficial animals and insects as well as the targeted pest. Organic chemical controls should be considered only as a last resort.

The following gives some useful information about the most common pests and diseases we deal with at RBGE and the most effective ways of controlling them.

Mice

Damage – eat and damage young pea, bean and beetroot seeds and seedlings

Other signs – small holes in soil/compost

Control methods

- Cover seeds and seedlings with a mesh cage or plastic lid.
- Sow susceptible crops in pots or modules positioned above ground level on a table. Plant out once they are well established.
- Sow seeds surrounded by prickly leaves (holly, gorse). Or deter with strong smells, for example coat seeds with ginger or chai tea.
- Trap mice.

Badgers ▼

Damage – holes and soil disturbance through digging for worms; they also eat some crops, such as carrots and onions

Other signs – turf dug up around vegetable plots

Control method

- Deter with human presence, radio noise, cat's eyes, or in extreme cases set up an electric fence. Badgers are powerful creatures and can get through most barriers.

Pigeons ▲

Damage – decimate young and established brassicas and peas

Other signs – onions pulled out of the soil

Control methods

- Cover plants with fleece or open mesh to prevent attack.
- Use anything that scares the birds – a sudden sound, flickering light or motion, old CDs suspended from canes, a child's windmill, a scarecrow or a thin plastic tape stretched between two poles which vibrates in the wind.

Carrot root fly

Damage – larvae burrow into carrots damaging roots and this often leads to other secondary infections

Other signs – difficult to see damage until crops are harvested; can affect all plants in the Apiaceae family

Control methods

- Cover plants with fleece or surround carrots with a high-sided barrier (approximately 50cm). Carrot flies are low flying.
- Sow sparsely to avoid later thinning, which can release a scent that attracts carrot flies.
- Sow early to avoid the first laying phase of carrot flies (late May/June).
- Biological nematode control is available.

© Visuals Unlimited/Corbis

Cabbage root fly ▲

Damage – larvae eat roots and kill the plant

Other signs – plants keel over or wilt

Control methods

- Cover plants completely with fine mesh/ fleece to prevent flies from gaining access to soil around plants. Alternatively, cover soil surrounding stalks with fabric or cardboard (cabbage collar) to prevent eggs being laid in the soil.
- Encourage natural predators (birds) or mask brassica smells with companion planting.
- Biological nematode control is available.

Aphids

Damage – black, green, yellow, red and grey coloured, sap-sucking insects distort leaf growth, weaken plant growth and spread viruses

Other signs – aphids secrete a liquid sugar (honeydew) that can cause a secondary problem of sooty mould; ants are also a good indicator of aphid presence as they patrol and protect the aphids to harvest their honeydew

Control methods

- Prevent soft new growth with correct feeding and watering. Pinch out soft growth (broad beans) if appropriate.
- Remove aphids by squashing or blasting off with a spray of water.
- Use sticky traps in indoor environments as indicators of aphid levels.
- Encourage natural predators (blue tits, hoverflies, ladybirds and parasitic wasps).
- Grow plants that are more desirable to aphids as a decoy, for example, nasturtium.
- Spray with a soft soap-and-water solution.

Caterpillars (cabbage white and small cabbage white butterflies) ▲

Damage – eat large holes or strip brassica leaves completely

Other signs – yellow eggs laid on the underside of leaves

Control methods

- Check the underside of leaves and remove eggs and caterpillars by hand.
- Encourage birds (robins and blackbirds) that will prey on caterpillars.
- Expose pest through soil cultivation.
- Cover plants with fine mesh to prevent contact with butterflies and moths.
- Use bacterium *Bacillus thuringiensi*, which is harmless to other beneficial insects.

Pea moth ▼

Damage – larvae eats peas inside the pod

Other signs – exit holes in peas and pods

Control methods

- Protect crop with fine mesh barrier to prevent moths laying eggs on flowers.
- Grow early- or late-cropping peas to avoid moth egg-laying period.
- Tolerate a few damaged peas.

© Nigel Cattlin/Visuals Unlimited/Corbis

Flea beetle ▲

Damage – numerous tiny holes on leafy crops, often brassicas

Other signs – jumping insects when plants are touched or soil is disturbed

Control methods

- Avoid dry soil conditions that are conducive to flea beetles.
- Avoid growing susceptible plants or learn to accept some crop damage. Unless damage is severe it will not harm the plant but will just look unsightly.
- Cover a card with petroleum jelly and move it slowly over the top of the crop. The flea beetles will hop up and stick to the card.
- Cover with a fine mesh after sowing to prevent flea beetles from entering.

Vine weevil ▲

Damage – plants wilt suddenly because of vine weevil larvae eating root system

Other signs – vine weevil adults leave notch marks in leaves on specific plants.

Control methods

- Break the cycle by collecting adult vine weevil when they are active at night by using a torch.
- Use a sacrificial plant to lure vine weevils away from other crops; they love cyclamen.
- Check for larvae in early spring around roots, destroy them and re-pot plants.
- Water nematode *Steinernema kraussei* into soil when temperatures are above 5°C.

www.picturenation.co.uk

Red spider mites ▶

Damage – yellowing of leaves, fine webbing on underside of leaves

Other signs – mites are invisible to the naked eye so hard to detect

Control methods

- Create high humidity by 'damping down' indoor environments on hot days.
- Use the predatory mite *Phytoseiulus persimilis* to control infestation when temperatures are above 16°C.

Slugs and snails ▲

Damage – defoliate and weaken plants. Often notches are removed from leaves or seedlings are eaten back to stalks.

Other signs – silvery trails

Control methods

- Avoid creating succulent plant growth through overfeeding.
- Remove potential hiding places (dark, damp conditions, leaf litter and debris) to expose pests and their eggs to predators.
- Attract natural predators (hedgehogs, frogs, toads and birds).
- Water nematode *Phasmarhabditis hermaphrodita* into soil when temperature is above 5°C.
- Surround plants with coarse materials such as grit, eggshells, soot or coffee grounds.
- Copper bands/tapes around plants will give slugs and snails a small electric charge.
- Chemical baits are available but most are toxic to vertebrates.
- Collect slugs and snails at night with a torch when they are most active.
- Sow seed indoors and plant out when the plants are big enough to withstand damage.

Diseases

Diseases can be caused by fungi, bacteria or viruses.

Clubroot

Damage – plants wilt and die suddenly

Other signs – white growths found on roots of brassicas

Control methods

- Practice crop rotation.
- Raise the soil pH, as fungi thrive in low pH (acidic) conditions.
- Ensure soil is well drained.
- Grow clubroot-resistant cultivars (such as cauliflower 'Clapton').
- Start off young brassicas indoors to give them the best start.

Consider growing a different crop family if your plot is badly affected, as clubroot can live in the soil for 20 years.

Damping off ▼

Damage – seeds fail to germinate or seedlings collapse and die

Other signs – stems of seedlings appear thin near the soil.

Control methods

- Sow thinly or into modules to prevent fungal spores spreading.
- Avoid watering from overhead as water droplets can spread the disease.
- Ensure seedlings have adequate ventilation.
- Prick out healthy plants into modules to prevent further spread.

© Nigel Cattlin/Visuals Unlimited/Corbis

Grey mould ▲

Damage – grey/brown fluffy mould on leaves or fruits; often worse in humid and damp conditions. Common in greenhouse and polytunnel culture where there is poor ventilation.

Control methods
- Ensure adequate air circulation and avoid watering from overhead.
- Remove infected plant parts to avoid further spread.
- Fungicides are available.

Powdery mildew

Damage – plants covered with a fine white powder. Certain plants are particularly susceptible (courgettes, cucumbers, strawberries).

Control methods
- Correct spacing to allow good airflow around plants.
- Ensure plants are adequately watered and soil does not become dry.
- Remove affected leaves to minimise spread to other plants.
- Use sulphur smoke to restrict spread.

Rusts ◢

Damage – small yellow, rust or brown coloured spots. Often more unsightly than causing any real damage. Tend to be crop-specific (leeks, onions, mint).

Control methods
- Avoid nitrogen-rich soils.
- Remove infected leaves, clean equipment to avoid contamination, practise crop rotation.
- Tolerate a small amount of damage unless crop yields are significantly affected.

Chocolate spot

Damage – brown spots on leaves (specific to broad beans)

Control methods
- Leave unless the problem is affecting plant growth; it is unlikely to harm plant growth significantly except in very bad cases.
- Remove infected material and do not compost.

Potato and tomato blight ▲

Damage – brown freckles or lesions appear on foliage and stems. Plants shrivel and die back quickly, tubers turn to mush and fruits rot.

Control methods
- Grow resistant varieties (such as potato 'Sarpo mira') and always buy certified seed stock.
- Water beneath foliage to avoid spraying it.
- Grow tomatoes indoors to give some protection from blight spores.
- If plants are believed to be infected, cut back potato stems (haulms) to ground level to prevent infection spreading to potato tubers under the soil. Lift potatoes and use quickly.
- Dispose of infected material carefully, ensuring it is not incorporated into the composting system. Remove all tubers as these can leave a reservoir of spores in the ground for the future.

Viruses ▲

There are hundreds of different viruses that can affect plants. Most are specific to particular crops but very difficult to identify. Common ones include lettuce, cucumber, radish and aubergine mosaic virus and carrot red-leaf virus.

Damage – stunted or distorted growth, mottling on leaves, generally weak plant growth

Other signs – aphids present; they are often the vector transmitting the virus between plants

Control methods
- Buy certified virus-free stock.
- Cover plants with fine mesh or horticultural fleece to prevent insect contact.
- Remove infected plants and do not compost.
- Remove weeds in the same plant family that may continue to host the virus.
- Use sticky traps to monitor aphid presence and levels.

Common disorders

Nutrient deficiencies

Nitrogen deficiency

Damage – growth stunted, leaves turn yellow then red or purple; this is caused by poor soil condition

Control methods
- Maintain healthy soil by adding plenty of organic matter prior to planting.
- Grow and dig in green manure.
- Apply high-nitrogen fertilisers (chicken manure).

Potassium deficiency

Damage – leaves curl and develop purple or brown margins. Lack of potassium causes poor fruit and flower development. It can also lead to a disorder known as greenback on tomatoes (see 'High temperatures', p. 75).

Control method
- Apply high potassium feed (tomato feed).

Phosphorous deficiency

Damage – leaves turn bluish-purple and brown

Control method
- Apply phosphorous fertilisers, such as bone meal, before planting.

Magnesium deficiency

Damage – yellowing between leaf veins. Caused by acidic soils or the presence of excessive potassium.

Control methods
- Check soil pH and adjust accordingly.
- Apply a foliar feed containing magnesium (Epsom salts, or nettle or comfrey tea solution).

Calcium deficiency

Damage – often crop specific. Patches of brown or green-black at the base of ripening tomatoes and peppers, known as blossom end rot, are caused by low levels of calcium or a lack of water preventing the uptake of calcium.

Control methods
- Ensure adequate water and avoid fluctuations in moisture.
- Check soil pH and adjust accordingly.

Common cultural conditions

High temperatures

Damage – plants wilt and leaves curl, especially under glass. High temperatures can also lead to problems with pollination and cause disorders like greenback on tomatoes. Greenback stops fruit from ripening, leaving a hard green surface at one side. Outside crops are more prone to bolt in high temperatures.

Control methods

- Ensure plants are not subjected to extremes of temperature by ensuring adequate ventilation and shading, especially indoors.
- Provide adequate water and damp down indoor spaces to reduce high temperatures.
- Grow resistant varieties: 'Moneymaker' and 'Tigerella' tomatoes show resistance to greenback.

Frost damage ▸

Damage – die back of plants (brown or blackening of leaves or petals)

Control methods

- Cover with fleece or another form of protection.
- Avoid planting in frost pockets.
- Work back from last likely frost dates in your area and sow accordingly to avoid damage (see frost date table p. 6).

Excessive water

Damage – too much water can lead to poor root growth and rotting. Sudden amounts of moisture can also cause fruits and roots to split (tomatoes, carrots).

Control methods

- Prevent over watering by providing good drainage (incorporate grit/sand on heavy soils).
- Ensure good soil husbandry by adding plenty of organic matter to provide good water-holding capacity.

Lack of water

Damage – flowers may fail to set fruits (runner beans), plants bolt. Poor fruit set is also caused by a lack of humidity on indoor plants (tomatoes, cucumbers).

Control methods

- Spray indoor crops (tomatoes, cucumbers) with water or damp down polytunnel/greenhouse floor to create humid environment.
- Ensure adequate watering.
- Incorporate organic matter prior to planting to ensure good water-holding capacity of soil.
- Mulch plants to lock in available moisture.

Wind damage

Damage – leaf tips and flowers become brown and shrivelled where they are burnt by the wind. Plants can also be knocked down and damaged by wind.

Control methods

- Create some form of windbreak (see p. 5).
- Provide adequate supports and stake taller crops.
- Avoid planting out too early.

At RBGE we encourage natural predators such as ladybirds, hoverflies, lacewings, ground beetles, centipedes, spiders, wasps, frogs and toads. This is achieved by creating diverse habitats in and around the plots.

Weeding

It is important to control weeds as they compete with your plants for water, nutrients and light and can be a reservoir for pests and diseases. However, weeds can be attractive, some are edible and they provide food for insects and birds.

Know your weeds

There are two weed groups:

- Annuals – their lifecycle (germination, growth and flowering) takes place in less than one year
- Perennials – their lifecycle is longer than one year

It is good practice to learn to identify weed seedlings so that you recognise them in their early stages and understand the best strategy for removal.

Common weeds

Annual	Perennial
Annual meadow grass	Bindweed
Chickweed	Bramble
Fat hen	Couch grass
Goose grass, cleavers, sticky willy	Creeping buttercup
Groundsel	Creeping thistle
Hairy bittercress	Dandelion
Himalayan balsam	Docks
Pearlwort	Giant hogweed
Poppies	Ground elder
Ragwort	Japanese knotweed
Shepherd's purse	Nettles
	Rosebay willowherb

General control techniques

Perennial weeds

Try to eliminate perennial weeds before cultivating as they are difficult to remove once crops are growing.

- Remove roots and top growth with a trowel or hand fork. Continual removal will weaken growth.
- Suppress weeds by covering them with cardboard or plastic to weaken plant growth. This may take time but is well worth doing on badly infested areas.
- In severe cases chemicals may help to bring persistent weeds under control. A translocated herbicide (e.g. glyphosate) will be absorbed through the leaves and to the roots.
- Target weeds only as the chemical kills all plants. Follow the manufacturer's guidelines.
- Learn to live with a few of the weeds. Many weedy plants can be eaten (ground elder, dandelions, nettles).
- Avoid rotavating perennial weeds as they can regenerate from small pieces of root.

Annual weeds

- After preparing a seed bed, wait for a couple of weeks for weeds to germinate, then hoe off seedlings before sowing crops. (Newly prepared soil can be covered with clear plastic to encourage annual weed germination.)
- Help break the weed cycle by removing weeds before they set seed.
- Use a sharp hoe, little and often, when weeds are young. Hoe in dry weather so that seedlings dry out quickly.
- Hand weeding after rain allows the roots to be pulled out easily.
- Mulch around crops (with plastic sheeting, grass clippings, newspaper or compost) to suppress weed germination.
- Grow crops very densely in close rows or patches (lettuce, carrots) to outcompete weed growth, or leave space between rows to allow weeds to be hoed.

Mulching is an effective technique used in conjunction with hand weeding and hoeing for annual weeds. Covering the soil around your plants with composted organic material will help to suppress weeds, lock in moisture and supply a slow release of nutrients to your vegetables. If you use your own garden compost it is also free.

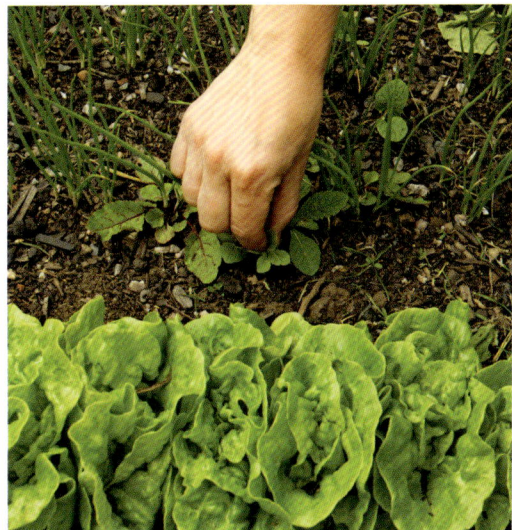

Composting

A compost heap is an essential part of a vegetable garden. Growing edible crops every year in the same space will deplete the soil of nutrients. Composting is a great way of recycling nutrients to return them to the ground.

Compost:

- Improves soil structure and helps it hold water.
- Helps moderate the pH.
- Reduces waste going to landfill.
- Is a great alternative to synthetic fertilisers, which require a lot of energy to produce.

What to compost

Successful compost is made from a balance of 50 per cent green waste and 50 per cent brown waste. A compost heap will also need water and should be moist but not sodden.

Green waste	Brown waste
Nitrogen-rich, wet material	Carbon-rich, dry material
Vegetable peelings including potato peelings	Woody prunings (anything thicker than your thumb needs to be cut up or shredded)
Leafy garden trimmings	Scrunched-up paper
Rhubarb and other poisonous plants can be used	Eggshells (these should be added with caution as they take a very long time to break down)
Grass cuttings (add with brown waste to prevent the mix getting sloppy)	Cardboard, such as egg cartons and toilet roll tubes
Foliage from potatoes if blight free	Hay

Do not compost:

- Cooked foods
- Animal waste
- Bones and meat scraps
- Perennial weeds (unless killed first by leaving in the sun or in water)
- Large quantities of wood shavings
- Coal or charcoal ash

Hot composting

Heat, generated by bacteria, gets trapped and leads to fast composting. This has the advantage of killing weeds and seeds but it requires a larger heap to generate the heat required. The heap should contain at least one cubic metre of material added all at once. The mix requires turning weekly to provide aeration and prevent the compost becoming too hot. Large timber bay bins work well for this and if you have space it is useful to have two or three at different stages of development.

Cold composting

Plastic bins can be used for cold composting and you can add materials gradually as you accumulate them; it will, however, take a lot longer. Place your bin directly on the soil to enable composting organisms to get into it. A good heap will be alive with micro-organisms; worms and even slugs are beneficial in this environment.

Leaves

Decomposed leaves are a valuable addition to home-made compost, adding structure. Compost leaves separately as they take a long time to decompose and slow the process; mix them with compost when both are broken down. Collect leaves and store them in a cage constructed from four posts and chicken wire. Alternatively put them in black bin bags, water them and pierce holes in the sides. Leave these to break down; it will take two to three years.

At the Edinburgh Garden we compost waste material in large open mounds called windrows. Because of their size the heaps heat up and thermophilic (heat-loving) micro-organisms speed up the composting process. We add fresh horse manure from the Fettes police stables. This arrangement has worked successfully for over a decade. We also add decomposed leaf mould or finely graded composted woodchip to the mix before sifting, to create a lovely crumbly texture.

Seasonal tasks

Keeping your garden producing all year round relies on you working with the conditions. We have divided the year up seasonally to give you an idea of what to expect, when jobs should be tackled and what to look out for.

Spring

March, April, May

Growing conditions

With the return of longer days and warmer temperatures, spring is the key time for sowing. Draw up a calendar of sowing times using pp. 32–35. A long and successful harvest will depend on being organised and planning ahead.

Be aware that spring arrives later the further north you go. Seed packets suggest a range of times for sowing; it is worth experimenting but in Scotland start a few weeks into the range given. Keep an eye on the weather forecast; a warm spell will bring sowing dates forward. If unseasonal frosts threaten you can cover tender spring growth, such as early potato shoots, with fleece or other forms of protection.

Sowing and planting

- Before sowing you will need to make final preparations to your soil. The aim is a fine 'tilth', a crumbly soil structure ideal for germinating seeds.
- It is possible to warm the soil a few weeks before sowing by covering it with cloches or black plastic (see p. 59).

Sow a range of crops outdoors from March onwards (see Calendar, pp. 32–35 for specific crop information) but delay sowing until April if the weather is cold. As seeds germinate, thin out seedlings to the required spacing. Crops can be started off early on a windowsill, in a cold frame, greenhouse or polytunnel, or under cloches.

Plant out seed potatoes but cover the new growth with soil to prevent tubers forming on the surface of the soil where light exposure can make them toxic. This is called 'earthing up'. Sow and plant out tender vegetables such as courgettes, runner beans and French beans by the end of May.

'Harden off' plants that are being moved into the garden from protected cultivation. This means slowly acclimatising them to the lower temperature and windier conditions they will face outside.

Harvesting

- Harvest overwintering vegetables.
- Lift crops that have been in the ground all winter, such as leeks and parsnips, so that they don't begin to resprout.

Watch out for

- Weeds – during the seedling stage vegetables are susceptible to being swamped by weeds; hoe and hand-weed carefully around young plants
- Slugs – they can quickly demolish young plants
- Mice – they eat freshly planted beans and peas. Take steps to protect seedlings (see p. 69).

To do

- Mulch with a layer of well-rotted compost when seedlings are established to discourage weeds and prevent water loss.
- Erect bean poles and other supports before planting seedlings out (see p. 63).

Summer

June, July, August

Growing conditions

Long hours of daylight and warm sunshine mean rapid growth for crops, but this goes for weeds too. Periods of drought and rain at this time can badly affect some crops. Growing a wide range of crops increases the chances of success. Sowing small batches of quick-growing plants at regular intervals minimises the risk of losing the whole crop to inclement weather; this also helps to extend your harvest period (see p. 26).

Sowing and planting

- June is the last chance to plant out tender crops such as tomatoes and runner beans.
- Continue to sow peas until July.
- Plant out winter brassicas in June.
- Plant 'early' seed potatoes to provide a crop of new potatoes late in the year.
- Winter salads can be sown directly outside.
- Sow spring cabbage seeds in August.

Harvesting

- This is the start of the peak harvesting time; pick regularly to prevent crops becoming too big.
- Remove any plants that have bolted and replace them with quick-growing crops such as salad greens and radishes.
- In August lift and dry onions and garlic.

Watch out for

- Weeds – they grow rapidly at this time of year; regular hoeing is the best solution
- Caterpillars – especially on brassicas

To do

- Protect brassicas from birds.
- Thin out seedlings.
- Watering – keep an eye on the weather and ensure nothing dries out.
- Pinch out tomato side shoots.
- Feed potatoes and tomatoes.
- Shade and ventilate the greenhouse.
- Water the path and benches of your greenhouse to reduce heat and keep the atmosphere moist.
- Turn your compost heap and water it if necessary.

Autumn

September, October, November

Growing conditions

Plant growth stalls as temperatures fall and daylight hours diminish. Only a select group of vegetables will be able to germinate at this time of year and survive the colder months. The first frosts usually arrive in October in Scotland.

Sowing and planting

- September is your last chance to sow winter salads.
- Plant out spring cabbages.
- Sow hardy peas and beans to overwinter and provide an early crop next year.
- Plant garlic and autumn onions on free-draining soils.
- If crops finish early use the ground to sow quick-growing and overwintering green manures (crops that can be worked back into the soil to replace nutrients; see p. 40).

Harvesting

- Harvest and store crops as they mature.
- Collect and save seeds for next year (see p. 48).
- Clamp root crops (see p. 66).
- Make notes on what has grown well for next year.

Watch out for

- Fungi – especially in damp and humid conditions. Provide adequate ventilation in greenhouses and polytunnels and remove any infected growth as soon as you see it.
- Mould – on stored crops

To do

- Net all brassicas to protect from hungry pigeons.
- Continue feeding tomatoes until the crop is over.
- Mulch plants that will overwinter in the soil.
- Mulch bare ground to minimise damage to the soil during winter.
- Protect plants with cloches.
- Clean out and wash greenhouses to maximise available sunlight and remove overwintering pests.
- If possible insulate greenhouses and polytunnels.
- Reduce watering and ventilation in greenhouses.
- Insulate pots being left out for winter.
- Dig over plots as they become vacant and cover with plastic or weighted-down cardboard to prevent weeds (although this can provide shelter for slugs).

Winter

December, January, February

Growing conditions

This is the most limited time of year for plant growth. However, some plants are able to remain dormant and provide harvests, such as parsnips, swedes, some brassicas and winter and oriental greens.

Sowing and planting

- Sow hardy broad beans.
- Sow peas in guttering.
- Start some crops under heat or under cover.
- Sprout seeds on windowsills.
- Chit early potatoes.
- Grow herbs indoors, such as basil and coriander.
- Sow onion seed.

Harvesting

- Pick Brussels sprouts, leeks, parsnips, turnips and winter salads.
- Check stored vegetables regularly for rot.

Watch out for

- Overwintering snails and hungry pigeons; they are particularly attracted to brassicas.

To do

- Clean and clear out polytunnels, greenhouses, cold frames, pots and containers.
- Feed the birds – they might eat some slugs while they're there!
- Keep on top of any winter-germinating weeds.

Planning

- Plan next year's plot, decide what to grow and do research.
- Reassess your garden design in light of successes and failures from previous years.
- Order seed, seed potatoes and onion sets.

Preparation

- Dig over beds when they are not frozen.
- Add organic matter and mulch.
- Apply slow-release fertilisers.
- Add lime if necessary.
- Prepare trenches for runner beans.
- Cover the soil with black plastic or fleece to warm before sowing.

Maintenance

- Tidy up the shed.
- Check the soil for missed potatoes that could re-sprout.
- Insulate garden taps and hosepipes.
- Clear snow off polytunnels.
- Stake tall brassicas and other taller plants to prevent wind damage.

What to grow with children

Here are some ideas to get young gardeners outside and interested in growing their own food.

- **Cress heads**
  Children like things they can grow and eat quickly. Make these in empty painted egg shells. Fill the shells with damp cotton wool and a generous amount of cress seeds. Keep them in a bright place and water regularly; in a week or so you can give them a haircut!

- **Pizza pot**
  Grow your pizza ingredients all together. Plant out tomatoes, basil, oregano, rocket and even onion sets or spring onions in a large pot. Make sure the tomatoes have support and plenty of sun to ripen them. Then simply harvest and add cheese!

- **Fun containers**
  Let your children decorate some containers with paint. Remember anything can make a good plant pot so long as it has drainage holes in the bottom. Recycle yoghurt pots, ice-cream tubs and plastic bottles.

- **Potatoes**
  There is nothing more satisfying than growing potatoes and harvest time always feels like the excitement of a lucky dip. Children love the varieties with blue-purple flesh such as 'Salad Blue' or 'Shetland Black'. Try using an old dustbin; make holes in the bottom and larger ones in the sides. Plant potatoes in layers up the bin at the same height as the holes and water well. The plants will grow out of the holes, and when it is time to harvest you can dig them in layers or empty everything out and root through it together.

- **Chives**
  These are perennials and can be split each year to make new plants. They are a favourite for children to munch on during gardening sessions.

- **Jack and the beanstalk**
  Runner beans can be grown up a wall or over an archway. Use bamboo to make a frame in the shape of your choice and plant young plants at the bottom. Train them over your shape and then pick them together from all heights and overhead.

Tips when growing with children

- Leave a small digging area for young children where they can practise using tools and hunt for mini beasts.

- Children love digging holes but when sowing seeds they only need to make a shallow drill with a finger.

- A tip to save seeds is to practise sowing first on paper. Turn it into a game with younger children and get them to make letters or shapes. Remember that when you sow in the soil you should do so in straight rows so you will know which plants are weeds.

- Make sure your children understand what is and is not edible, and ensure they wash their hands after digging.

- Choose crops that are easy to grow. We suggest radishes, beetroot, spring onions, lettuces and sugar snap peas.

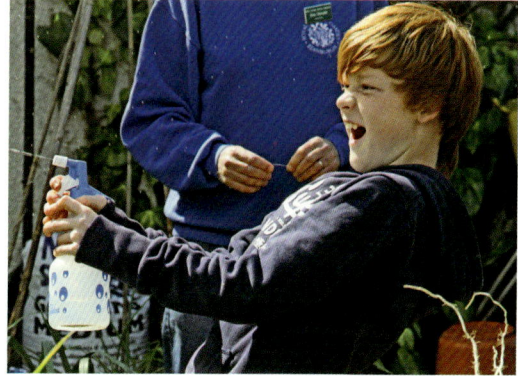

School Gardening Project

RBGE have been gardening with children since 1983. Currently we have five plots looked after by children from local primary, secondary and special schools. Each child has their own small area within the plot and a system called 'square foot gardening' is used, where crops are grown intensively in a small space. We maximise this space by sowing alternate drills of root and leaf crops, a good way of getting children to think about what part of the plant they eat!

Vegetable varieties are chosen according to their small size, ease of growing in Scotland's climate, strange colour (purple carrots are very popular!) and taste. The children often want to eat things they have grown straight away but also take home their harvests to share with their families.

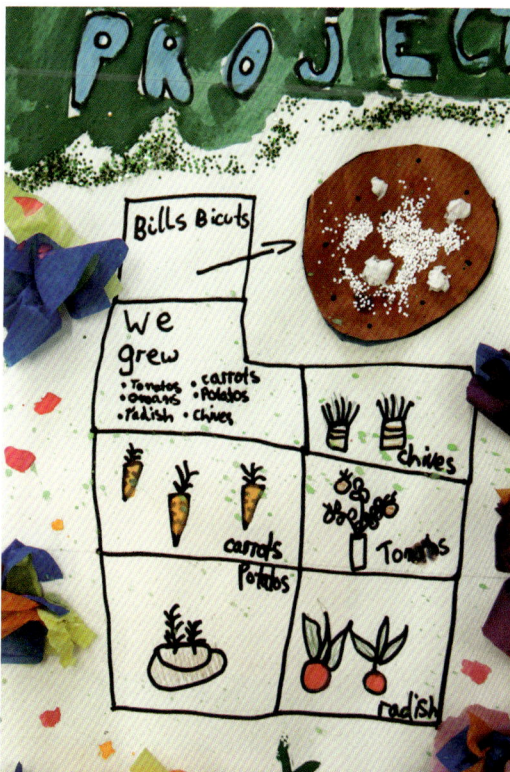

The Edible Gardening Project

RBGE's mission is to 'explore and explain the world of plants for a better future' and we achieve this through our work in horticulture and botany, conservation, research, education and public programmes. The Garden teamed up with the Scottish Allotments and Gardens Society (SAGS) in 2011 for the community-focused Edible Gardening Project, contributing to our mission.

Growing food has become more popular in recent years, with seed companies and garden centres reporting rocketing sales, and people on allotment waiting lists in Edinburgh for up to nine years. Despite this SAGS has found that many people give up their long-awaited allotments within the first two years because they lack basic horticultural knowledge. The Edible Gardening Project was designed to help overcome this problem. Funded by Players of People's Postcode Lottery and based at the Edinburgh Garden, it aims to share horticultural knowledge, skills and enthusiasm for growing food with diverse communities.

The project was an instant hit, with thousands of people coming to learn and to seek advice. A group of dedicated volunteers, recruited specifically for the project, worked hard to develop the demonstration Edible Garden. They were also on hand at regular workshops and drop-in sessions to provide support and advice to visitors. The plots and polytunnel have proved a popular addition and provide an excellent opportunity to showcase edible plants, including crops suitable for overwintering in Scotland. In addition the project has worked with local community projects, offering practical assistance and workshops.

Community gardening

Many people enjoy the benefits of involvement in community gardening projects nationally. A recent study* has shown that they improve people's access to fresh healthy food and provide an opportunity to spend more time outside doing physical activities. The gardens also offer an opportunity for socialising and being part of a group. Even just being able to view green space has been shown to reduce stress.** Community projects allow participants to grow their own food even if they don't have space for their own garden and the allotment waiting list is full.

Volunteering

- There are all sorts of organisations and individuals looking for help in the garden. Get creative and garden without a garden by looking for opportunities at local volunteering organisations.

- Find your local community garden and see if they are looking for help. There is a vast network of projects all over the country in urban and rural areas.

- Don't wait for someone else – start your own community garden.

What our volunteers have said

"Volunteering fills me up with what I need as far as going back to nature goes. To give something back and to work in the gardens, it's just an absolute pleasure." **Mary**

"I love gardening and I love being outdoors. I've always loved the Botanic Gardens. It is also a great way for me to learn about growing vegetables." **Jan**

"Volunteering will allow me to develop the skills I need to grow my own vegetables. I can come here to learn and then share my new skills." **Laura**

* True Value Report, Federation of City Farms and Community Gardens.
** *Health Benefits of Gardens in Hospitals*, Roger S. Ulrich, 2002.

Recipes, tips and interviews

Always wash any vegetables you pick before cooking. Be sure you have identified all flowers and plant parts accurately. Be aware of any allergies before serving.

Peanutty spinach

Volunteer Jane Raymond supplied us with this one. "It's a recipe I got from Tanzania but it's popular all over East Africa; quick, easy and yummy."

> 1 tbsp olive oil
>
> 1 large onion, chopped
>
> 5 medium/large tomatoes, chopped
>
> 100–150g spinach
>
> 1–2 tbsp peanut butter
>
> Ground black pepper
>
> Chilli powder or cayenne pepper

- Fry the onion with the tomatoes in the oil until the mixture has a sauce-like consistency (about 10 minutes).
- Add the spinach (you can use chard or any green leaves but if using anything large it's better to chop it before adding).
- Cook for a couple of minutes then add peanut butter to your taste.
- Season with pepper and a pinch of chilli powder or cayenne pepper depending on how spicy you like it.
- Serve with rice.

Spicy beetroot, tomato and carrot soup

Edible Gardening Project Community Gardener Ben has used this recipe after a beetroot glut. Beetroot is an easy crop to grow but you can easily become overwhelmed if you sow too many. The soup can be frozen.

> 2 tbsp sunflower oil
>
> 1 onion, finely chopped
>
> 2 or 3 carrots, coarsely grated
>
> 3 or 4 medium-sized beetroots, coarsely grated
>
> 2 cloves garlic, crushed
>
> 1 tsp smoked sweet paprika
>
> 1 tsp ground cumin seeds
>
> 1 tsp ground coriander seeds
>
> ½ tsp ground cinnamon
>
> ¼ tsp cayenne pepper
>
> 1 tin tomatoes (or fresh if you have them)
>
> 1 tbsp tomato puree
>
> 1 litre of vegetable stock or water
>
> Sour cream, finely chopped fresh coriander leaves and pepper to serve

- Heat the oil over a medium heat and sweat the onions, carrots, beetroots and garlic for 10–15 minutes.
- Increase the heat, add the spices and stir well for 2–3 minutes.
- Add the tinned tomatoes, tomato puree and stock. Bring to the boil and simmer for 30 minutes or until all the vegetables are tender.
- Blend the soup until smooth.
- Serve with a spoonful of sour cream, a scattering of chopped coriander leaves and a grind of black pepper.

Nasturtium and parsley pesto

Edible Gardening Project Manager Jenny Foulkes made this welcome discovery after sowing the delightful orange flowers a bit too enthusiastically. Overwhelmed by a nasturtium forest, she found this recipe was perfect, especially as it can be frozen (before adding the pine nuts and parmesan cheese – you can add these later when defrosted). The quantities of ingredients can be changed to taste – lots of pesto recipes use much more oil but we found this enough.

> 1 cup nasturtium leaves
> (or substitute nasturtium for 2 cups spinach)
> 1 cup parsley leaves
> 1 garlic clove, crushed
> ½ cup olive oil
> 25g pine nuts or walnuts
> 50g parmesan cheese
> Juice of ½ a lemon
> Salt and black pepper to taste

- Wash leaves well and then blend all ingredients together. When the mixture is smooth it is ready to use.
- Stir into cooked pasta for a quick (and very green) meal.

Nadia's herby salad dressing

This recipe is very adaptable and goes well with a fresh green garden salad. It is particularly good with feta cheese and globe artichoke salad. You can use any herbs you like; the trick is to add three parts oil to two parts vinegar.

> Large handful of finely chopped garden herbs such as parsley, chives, dill and coriander
> 90ml walnut oil
> 60ml white wine vinegar
> 1 tbsp honey
> 1 tsp wholegrain mustard
> (can be substituted with chopped chilli or garlic)
> Salt and pepper

- Mix all ingredients well with an egg whisk.
- Drizzle over salad.

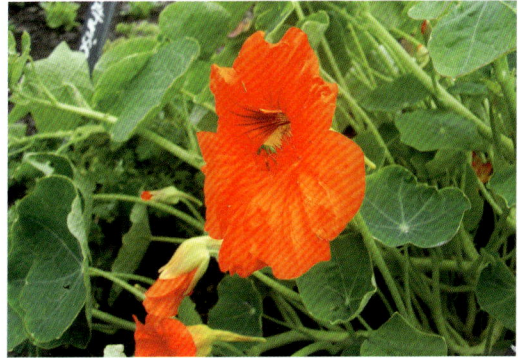

Courgette fritters

Edible Gardening Project volunteer Jan gave us this recipe. Courgettes can be very fruitful so a recipe that uses three at once is extremely useful.

For about 20 fritters:

> 3 small courgettes
> (coarsely grated and left in a tea-towel to reduce the water content for approximately 20 mins)
> 5 spring onions, finely chopped
> 250g feta cheese, crumbled
> Small bunch of parsley, chopped
> Small bunch of mint, chopped
> 1 tbs dried mint
> 1 tsp paprika
> Pepper (no salt needed)
> 140g plain flour
> 3 eggs, beaten
> Olive or vegetable oil for frying
> Lime to squeeze over finished fritters

- Put all ingredients except flour, eggs and courgettes in a bowl and mix thoroughly.
- Add the flour and beaten eggs and finally stir in the drained courgettes to produce a lumpy batter.
- Heat the oil and drop in dessertspoonfuls of batter, cooking each for approximately 2-4 minutes on one side.
- Flatten each to form a patty, then turn over and fry for 2 minutes on the other side. They are best light and fluffy inside and crisped on the outside.

Jenny Mollison, Scottish Allotments and Gardens Society Secretary

Jenny first grew vegetables when she was five, helping both her father and grandfather in the garden. On moving to a new house with a north-facing garden she was quick to sign up to the allotments located at the bottom of her garden. She has now had her own allotment for 24 years.

What were your first impressions of your allotment?

"I thought I had bitten off more than I could chew! It had been a bit neglected and perennial weeds had taken over; the couch grass was a real horror. I tackled it a little at a time, painstakingly teasing out the roots, unravelling it like a ball of string. I followed the roots under the soil and pulled them out very gently so they didn't snap off. I can spot the stuff a mile off now."

What has kept you interested?

"It's not just growing the fruit and vegetables; there is something really nice about getting down on your hands and knees and getting your hands in the soil. It is my little bit of nature, gardening away with the birds chattering in the trees. It's a stress buster and I get lost in it – my husband has to come and fetch me!"

Any advice for Scottish growers?

"Don't hurry; seed packets and television have you believe you can put everything in during March but you need to add two to four weeks in Scotland. We might have a shorter season but we do have long daylight hours, which is good for growing soft fruit."

> ❝ It's a stress buster and I get lost in it... ❞

David Knott, Associate Director of Horticulture, Royal Botanic Garden Edinburgh

David first started by helping his grandfather in his vegetable garden. He grew everything from Epicure potatoes to raspberries, a favourite to this day.

"The enjoyment of growing your own vegetables and fruit is unsurpassed. That's probably one of the reasons I got into horticulture – my grandfathers were both keen growers. That was out of necessity. Then there are all the health benefits not just in terms of diet but also the mental health benefits of being relaxed and growing your own fruit and veg; I don't think you can question that."

What is your advice for a beginner?

"To try, experiment. Ask advice locally – if you are on an allotment ask fellow allotment holders. I think you'll find that horticulturists by their nature are very free and open with their advice. It's not always an easy climate in Scotland – you can have late frosts, you can have cool springs, wet summers, early frosts; it can be quite frustrating. Watch the weather forecast and work with nature instead of against it."

"Children 'come alive' when they see their own plants growing..."

Cath Evans, Education Officer with the RBGE School Gardening Project

"Children 'come alive' when they see their own plants growing and gain confidence when they see the results of their labour. Even children who say they don't normally like vegetables try all kinds of things from strange-looking long white radishes to chive flowers to radish pods!"

"Gardening is a positive activity for all types of children from the shy and quiet to the 'can't sit still' energetic and has a focusing influence on all. Time slows down as working with the soil brings tiny discoveries of mini-beasts, seedlings and rogue potatoes. The joys and disappointments in the biodiversity of a flourishing or snail-ridden plot are shared by all."

Robyn Macdonald, Horticultural Technician

Robyn studied for a HND in Horticulture at RBGE before becoming a member of staff.

What did you learn from growing on the plots?

"I had very little previous experience of growing vegetables until I started on the student plot. It was my favourite part of the course. I got so much produce from one small plot. I harvested everything and put it all in the freezer. I made all sorts of things like carrot chutney and beetroot and chocolate brownies."

Are you still growing vegetables now?

"I don't have a garden at the moment but I grow tomatoes on my window ledge. It's a sunny spot so they do well. They smell great too."

> **" I got so much produce from one small plot…** I made all sorts of things like carrot chutney … and chocolate brownies. **"**

John Dunn, Senior Horticulturist, Edinburgh

"I started growing on one of the student plots at RBGE. That was only for one year and I'd caught the bug; my wife came up with the idea of square foot gardening at home, as we have a small garden. The idea of square foot gardening is just to sow what you are going to use and then sow again when you need more, rather than sowing the whole packet, and ending up with too much at once."

What is your biggest success?

"Potatoes – you can't go wrong with potatoes. We've grown potatoes in the square foot garden and in bags and pots as well. The ones in open ground are bigger than the ones in pots but they are perfect for salads."

What got you hooked?

"Growing your own produce, knowing what you are doing with it; that you're not using any chemicals and it's organic. It's hugely satisfying, and home-grown vegetables are definitely tastier; when you buy them from the supermarket they are really bland."

Tony Garn, Horticultural Supervisor

Tony Garn has worked at RBGE for 25 years and has always grown vegetables at home. His favourite crops are tomatoes, which he grows in a greenhouse directly in the soil, changing it every year to prevent the build-up of pests and diseases.

> " Keep a habitat heap: a pile of twigs, logs and sticks will encourage soil organisms and fauna. They will add to the overall health of a garden. "

"Value the soil; don't work it when it is wet…"

What tips would you give a beginner?

"Value the soil; don't work it when it is wet. If the soil builds up on the soles of your boots leave the job for another day; you'll be doing damage to the structure.

Don't be tempted to sow seed outside too early in Scotland. I wait until after Easter. If you sow into cold claggy soil you won't get a good germination rate.

Keep a habitat heap – a pile of twigs, logs and sticks will encourage soil organisms and fauna. They will all add to the overall health of a garden.

Always leave room in the vegetable garden for a tripod of sweet peas, then you will always have flowers to give as a gift."

Glossary

Bolt
Bolting is the term used when a plant flowers early. In edible plants this can be at the expense of the harvestable crop, as with leafy plants like lettuce, spinach and chard.

Bring on
When plants are manipulated in order to make them mature faster.

Chit (potatoes)
Chitting is the process of allowing seed potatoes to form shoots before planting. It is usual to chit the potatoes for 4–6 weeks in a cool place away from danger of frost. Somewhere light will discourage weak leggy shoots, but out of direct sunlight is best.

Coir
A growing medium made from coconut husks, which can be used as an alternative to peat in potting and seed compost.

Cultivar
A plant variety selected for a particular characteristic (usually bred in cultivation but sometimes occurring in the wild).

Damp down
Spraying water over paths and surfaces – usually in a polytunnel or greenhouse – in order to create a humid atmosphere.

Dibber
A pointed stick used to make holes in the soil when planting seeds or bulbs.

Earth up
The action of placing earth around the emerging stems and leaves of plants, particularly potatoes and leeks.

Etiolated
When plants grown in low light levels (especially seedlings) grow weak and leggy in an effort to reach sunlight.

Foliar feed
Liquid feed applied directly to leaves.

Harden off
The process of acclimatising plants to outdoor conditions. Usually plants grown indoors or in a greenhouse are placed outside for a few hours each day. The time outside is increased daily and after 1–2 weeks the plants are ready to go outside permanently.

Hungry gap
Refers to the time of year when the winter crops are finished, stored crops are used up and vegetables sown in spring are not yet ready.

Maincrop
Vegetable varieties/cultivars that produce a crop over a longer period during the main growing season (an alternative to early and late cropping varieties).

Modules
Seed trays with individual modular compartments.

Mulch
Refers to materials that are spread over the vegetable plot or around plants to improve soil, reduce water loss and suppress weeds. Materials can include wood chip, compost or weed matting.

Nematodes
Microscopic worms used as biological control for pests such as slugs and vine weevils.

Onion sets
Small onions in a juvenile state. These can be bought and planted out as an alternative to growing onions from seed.

Organic matter
Materials used to improve soil. This term refers to compost, well-rotted manure and green manures.

Overwinter
The act of keeping plants growing over the winter months. Some hardy plants can overwinter outside whilst others will benefit from protection from the elements.

Perennial
Plants that live for more than one year such as asparagus. Many vegetables are grown as annuals and only survive for one year, for example lettuce.

Pot bound
When a plant's roots become constricted within the pot and can no longer grow. This occurs when a plant is not 'potted on' into a larger pot.

Potager
The term 'potager' is French and means literally 'for the pot'. It refers to an ornamental kitchen garden. The aim of a potager is to make food production more attractive by growing vegetables and fruit interspersed with other plants such as annuals, herbs and grasses.

Seed leaves
Seed leaves are known botanically as cotyledons. They are the first leaves to emerge from the seed and often look different from the plant's mature leaves.

Seed viability
Refers to the ability of the seed to germinate. Seed viability reduces over time, how quickly depends on the species.

Successionally
Growing successionally is the process of sowing crops at regular intervals to ensure they are ready to harvest at different times, allowing for a continuous supply throughout the growing season.

Tilth
This term refers to the consistency of the soil structure. A fine tilth is a crumbly even texture of soil, with a small particle size suitable for sowing seeds.

True leaves
The leaves that appear after the seed leaves (cotyledons). They can identified by their shape, which is usually the same as the mature leaves of the plant.

Trug
Gardener's basket or bucket

Undercropping
Undercropping is a technique whereby smaller-sized plants are grown beneath larger and slower to mature crops. For example, lettuce might be grown below sweetcorn or climbing beans.

Vermiculite
Vermiculite is a heat-expanded mineral that is widely used in horticulture. It can be added to compost to improve structure for germinating seeds or used to cover very fine seeds when sowing, as it allows good light penetration. It also has good moisture and air-holding properties, which make it ideal for seed germination.

Acknowledgements

Images by:

Lynsey Wilson

Brenda White

Erica Randall

Helen Pugh

(images © Helen Pugh p. 11 bottom, p. 14 bottom, p. 24 bottom, p. 64 top left, p. 65, back cover top and middle insets)

Sadie Barber

Peter Clarke

Jenny Foulkes

The Royal Botanic Garden Edinburgh is grateful to all who have contributed to this book; in particular we would like to thank:

Players of People's Postcode Lottery

The Scottish Allotments and Gardens Society

Jenny Mollison

Brenda White

Anna Stevenson

David Knott

Cath Evans

Neil Woodcock

Jessica Roberts

The RBGE School Gardening Project Volunteers

Pupils from Flora Stevenson Primary School

The RBGE Edible Garden Volunteers

Hamish Adamson